Awareness of

The

Open Way

Pointers to Awakening

Based on the Meditations, Contemplations, and Experiences
of Forty Years of Spiritual Search and Practice
by Colin Drake

Copyright © 2013 by Colin Drake

ISBN: 978-1-304-50336-7

First Edition

All rights reserved. No part of this book shall be reproduced or transmitted, for commercial purposes, without written permission from the author.

Published by Beyond Awakening Publications, Tomewin

Cover design and photography by the author.

Also by the same author:

Beyond the Separate Self
The End of Anxiety and Mental Suffering

A Light Unto The Self
Self Discovery Through Investigation of Experience

Awakening and Beyond
Self-Recognition and its Consequences

Poetry
From Beyond The Separate Self

Poetry
From Being A Light Unto The Self

Humanity Our Place in the Universe
The Central Beliefs of the Worlds Religions

Poetry
From Awakening and Beyond

All of these titles are available as: e-books and in hard copy at
http://www.lulu.com/spotlight/ColinDrake

Contents

Introduction	4
Prologue – Awareness and Thought	16
1 The Open Way	21
2 Is Awareness The Absolute Reality?	26
3 Self-Referencing The 'Original Sin'	32
4 Analysis The Disease Not The Cure	39
5 Oneness	44
6 Loving 'What Is'	52
7 Ego Is Misidentification	59
8 The Myth of Ego	64
9 Why Write About The Ineffable?	68
10 The 'Problem' of Negative Thoughts	74
11 Handling Prejudice, Worldly and Racial	78
12 Awakening by Awareness of Awareness	83
13 Simplicity and Complexity	91
14 The Miraculous and The Auspicious	96
15 The Apparent Elasticity of Time	104
16 The Final Obstacle to Freedom	111
17 Awakening and Ethics	116
18 Staying Awake by The Bodhisattva Vow	122
19 Three Questions For Nondualists	129
20 Duality and Nonduality	137
21 The Seer, Knower and Enjoyer	145
22 The Question of 'Sin'	150
23 Two Modern Views of The Divine	156
24 The Fundamental Teachings of Buddhism	171
Appendix: Investigation of Experience	182
Addendum: Love Loving Itself	191
Spiritual Biography	202
Glossary	205
Bibliography	209
Index	211

Introduction

This book is written as a stand-alone guide to Awakening and is composed of articles written since the publication of *Awakening and Beyond*. At the time I thought that this would be the last book, so much so that I told someone that *Love Loving Itself* (chapter 23 in the above book) was my final word. It certainly felt like it at the time. But since then the questions, discussions and answers have continued resulting in this book. As I have said before I have no control over this process for I do not choose to sit and write articles, they just emerge from my meditations and contemplations or in response to questions and discussions. There are long periods when no writing takes place and then sometimes I can hardly stop!

To readers of my previous books the title of this one may look familiar but it has an extra element in an attempt to clearly redefine the term 'awareness' so that there can be no confusion. For recently I have realized that many people do not understand what I mean by this term, and this even applies to my previous readership. The confusion occurs due to the fact that there are two meanings of 'awareness', the limited (by the mind) and unlimited, the first being a partial version (or incidence) of the second. In what follows I have denoted the first by 'awareness' and the second by 'Awareness'. In general whenever I use this

Introduction

term I am meaning this second, apart from in the term 'awareness of Awareness' which includes them both. I hope this will be made clear in what follows:

'By observing mental states you also become aware of the seven factors of enlightenment. These are: awareness of Awareness, investigation of the Way, vigour, joy, serenity, concentration and equanimity.' (The Buddha, Maha Sattipatthana Sutta 14-16)

The first two are paramount and the last five are outcomes of these. This is what my books are all about, becoming 'aware of Awareness' through direct investigation and then continuing with further 'investigation of the Way' (the Tao, the nature of reality). I call this the Open Way for it is open to all and is a way to Awaken. The are many 'ways' but most of them are closed in that they require their adherents to have special knowledge, ability and discipline; whereas, awareness of Awareness is a simple direct seeing which when cultivated leads to full Awakening.

At this stage we need to become clear as to the meaning of the term 'awareness' which has two meanings which we must not confuse. The phrase 'awareness of Awareness' utilises both of these meanings and for this reason I have used a capital letter for the second one so that they may be easily distinguished in what follows.

The first occurrence (awareness) is synonymous with mindfulness, that is 'seeing' with the mind, or keeping (something) in the mind. It also means 'becoming conscious of', noticing, or perceiving, as in 'I became aware of …' This is the normal everyday usage as in the OED definition of 'aware' – *having knowledge or perception of ...*

So the term 'awareness of Awareness' means becoming conscious, or having knowledge or perception, of Awareness. We now need to define this Awareness which is simply the total 'seeing' and perceiving (or seer and perceiver) of everything detected by the mind and senses, whereas awareness (becoming aware of) is the partial 'seeing' of those thoughts/sensations on which the mind is focussed, or which are noticed. So these are not different, awareness just being a limited version (or incidence) of Awareness.

This is easy to directly experience by closing one's eyes and seeing whether you can simultaneously be 'aware of' (notice) all

Introduction

of the thoughts/mental images and sensations that are occurring. This is found to be impossible and yet these are all there in Awareness, which becomes apparent when one focuses one's mind on , or turns one's mind to, any of them…. and there they are! About this I wrote the following in *Beyond The Separate Sefl*:

> It is obvious that we would not 'know' (be aware of) our own perceptions without Awareness being present. This does not mean that we are always conscious of each one of them, as this is dictated by where we put our attention, or upon what we focus our mind. However, all sensations detected by the body are there in Awareness, and we can readily become conscious of them by turning our attention to them. It is also true that our thoughts and mental images immediately appear in Awareness, but these require less attention to be seen as they occur in the mind itself. So Awareness is like the screen on which all of our thoughts and sensations appear, and the mind becomes conscious of these by focusing on them. Take, for example, what happens when you open your eyes and look at a beautiful view: everything seen immediately appears in Awareness, but for the mind to make anything of this it

needs to focus upon certain elements of what is seen. 'There is an amazing tree', 'wow look at that eagle', 'what a stunning sky', etc. To be sure, you may just make a statement like 'what a beautiful view', but this does not in itself say much and is so self-evident as to be not worth saying!

The point is that the mind is a tool for problem-solving, information storing, retrieval and processing, and evaluating the data provided by our senses. It achieves this by focusing on specific sensations, thoughts or mental images that are present in Awareness, and 'processing' these. In fact we only truly see 'things as they are' when they are not seen through the filter of the mind, and this occurs when what is encountered is able to 'stop the mind'. For instance we have all had glimpses of this at various times in our lives, often when seeing a beautiful sunset, a waterfall or some other wonderful natural phenomenon. These may seem other-worldly or intensely vivid, until the mind kicks in with any evaluation when everything seems to return to 'normal'. In fact nature is much more vivid and alive when directly perceived, and

Introduction

the more we identify with the 'perceiver', as Awareness itself, the more frequently we see things 'as they are'. [1]

This Awareness is the constant conscious subjective presence in which our thoughts/mental images and sensations arise, abide, are spied and subside. Before every one of them Awareness is present, during each one of them they are 'seen' by This and This is still here after they go. Just check this out now – notice that before each thought/sensation there is Awareness of 'what is' (the totality of these at any given moment), during each of these there is Awareness of them within 'what is' and after each of them has gone there is still Awareness of 'what is'.

Rumi described this as: *the clear conscious core of your being, the same in ecstasy as in self-hating fatigue.* That is to say the Awareness in which the ecstasy or the self-hating fatigue appears. Now generally you would just be aware of, and affected by, the phenomenal state. If, however, you become aware of the Awareness in which this state is occurring and can fully identify with, and as, this Awareness then the state loses its power to affect your equanimity. For Awareness is always utterly still and

---

[1] C. Drake, *Beyond The Separate Self,* 2009, Tomewin, p.14-15.

Introduction

silent, totally unaffected by whatever appears in it, in the same way that the sky is unaffected by the clouds that scud across it.

It is this identification with Awareness that can be achieved by 'investigation of the Way' and the easiest way to do this is to directly investigate the nature of one's moment-to-moment experience, see the appendix. When this is successfully accomplished and you can see that at the deepest level, <u>you are Awareness itself</u> then this is an Awakening. If this cultivated by remaining 'aware of Awareness' (and identified as Awareness) then this leads to full Awakening.

The prologue is a reprint of an article which was actually entitled 'Awareness of Awareness' from *A Light Unto Your Self* and is reprinted here as it is a useful prelude to the material that follows.

Chapter one details how Awakening by becoming aware of (and identifying with) Awareness is an 'open' way not requiring any special esoteric knowledge or practices.

Introduction

Chapter two addresses the question of whether Awareness is the Absolute Reality and, regardless of the answer, whether there is anything that can be 'known' beyond this.

Chapter three discusses how 'self-referencing' that is how considering oneself as a separate object, and referring to oneself (mentally or verbally) as this, leads to unnecessary suffering.

Chapter four posits that continual self-analysis (identified with, or as, the mind) perpetuates the dis-ease of misidentification.

Chapter five attempts to show, in a logical and scientific framework, that everything (or no-thing!) in existence is of the same essence – Consciousness.

Chapter six addresses 'loving what is' - that is loving existence moment by moment as it actually 'is' and not as seen through by any filter of the mind, caused by ideology or misidentification.

Chapter seven discusses ego and shows how, by considering its various definitions, it is synonymous with misidentifying oneself as a separate object (in a universe of such).

Introduction

Chapter eight continues this theme to show that ego is actually a mythical entity. It also highlights the differences between ego and character, or personality, and posits that these two are necessary whereas the former is illusory.

Chapter nine was prompted by people questioning my motives for writing on the subject of Awakening and Awareness. It also came about when a friend posited that it's pointless attempting to put the ineffable into words.

Chapter ten was my response to the question of why the majority of thoughts appear to be negative.

Chapter eleven was in response to the same questioner who 'suffers' from worldly and racial prejudice and was asking how this could be addressed.

Chapter twelve is a hundred line poem dealing with overcoming mental suffering and misidentification by becoming aware of Awareness, the constant conscious subjective presence, and identifying with (and as) this.

Introduction

Chapter thirteen discusses the absolute simplicity of this method of Awakening and compares this with the many complex systems, ideologies and categories of (mis) identification which seem to appeal to the human mind.

Chapter fourteen considers humanity's fascination with the so-called miraculous and auspicious. It attempts to show that every moment is auspicious for Awakening and, once Awake, then everything is seen to be miraculous.

Chapter fifteen is an attempt to explain the apparent elasticity of time that is encountered after Awakening.

Chapter sixteen discusses the (apparent) 'final obstacle' to Awakening and the importance of one's thought processes in achieving freedom.

Chapter seventeen considers whether ethics are important in Awakening, or whether they are an outcome of this.

Chapter eighteen was written in response to a reader who had experienced 'Awakening' but whose mind continued to spin due to its lack of productive engagement with life.

Introduction

Chapter nineteen was stimulated by a nondualist who continued to take things personally, act defensively and engage with the world through the filter of his own knowledge.

Chapter twenty was written to address the apparent paradox of, or opposition between, duality and nonduality.

Chapter twenty one addresses three 'properties' of The Absolute, give in the Upanishads, those of Seeing, Knowing and Enjoying. It attempts to show that each of these may be used as a path to Self-realization.

Chapter twenty two considers the concept of 'sin' and offers a new definition of this which would apply equally well to all religions, tribes and cultures.

Chapter twenty three considers two modern views of the Absolute Reality by the mystic Georges Battaille and the feminist philosopher Luce Irigaray. It discusses the resonances between their views and those elucidated in previous chapters. It also compares their insights with those of the thirteenth century Christian mystic Marguerite Porete (the author of *The Mirror of*

Introduction

Simple Souls) and her peer the wonderful Sufi poet Jelaluddin Rumi.

Chapter twenty four explains the fundamental teachings of the Buddha, the four noble truths, and in this shows the resonances between these (teachings) and Awakening by becoming 'aware of Awareness'.

The appendix gives the basic format for investigating one's moment to moment experience which leads to the conclusion that, at the deepest level, one **is** Awareness.

The addendum has been added for it is a very useful practice to 'sense' and 'know' the Absolute – Consciousness – by using the body/mind as (its actual function) an instrument of This. The process has the advantage of never referencing the illusory 'small self' and thus cannot foster misidentification of oneself as a separate object.

If you have any questions on topics which are not covered in the text, or are not sure about those that are, you may contact me at colin108@dodo.com.au . Alternatively check out the contents of my other books at http://www.lulu.com/spotlight/ColinDrake

Prologue

Awareness and Thought

The following highlights the differences between thought and awareness and shows the importance of recognizing this.

Awareness and Thought

I recently received an e-mail from a reader who said they could not tell the difference between 'Awareness' and thought. I replied that I did not see how this was possible (please excuse my lack of acumen) and suggested that he consider the following:

(A) Thought	(The) Awareness
A 'sound' in the mind.	That which 'hears' this sound.
An object, some 'thing'.	The subject of this 'thing'.
The 'thing' that is witnessed.	The witness of this 'thing'.
The (thing that is) seen.	The seer.
A movement in the mind.	The aware stillness.
The (thing that is) known	The knower (of the thing).
That which comes & goes.	That which is always here.
An object of experience.	The experiencer.

Awareness and Thought

So Awareness is the constant conscious subjective presence which is aware of ephemeral objects (thoughts and sensations, mind and body) as they come and go.

'Awareness of Awareness' is the key to Awakening by the path of self-knowledge (Jnana), which is the most straightforward of the many paths available. Once one has become 'aware of Awareness' then Awakening is a direct result of this and the continuing investigation of this.

This is extremely simple, almost obvious, just the acknowledgement of the fact that one is aware of one's thoughts/mental images/sensations and that this Awareness is always present whereas thoughts/mental images/sensations come and go. The danger is that the mind will dismiss this as being too simple (and obvious) and therefore of no value. I urge you not to allow this, for if you do you will be overlooking the most precious realization. The mind naturally does this as it is not in its interests to acknowledge this recognition, for this will undermine its central dominant position.

Most people identify with their minds as being what they 'are' and this becoming 'aware of Awareness' has the potential to completely destroy this illusion. So the mind will try to negate this 'seeing'; the simple solution to this is, when it comes to reality, *don't believe a single thought.* Just rely on immediate direct experience, and this direct experience that you are Awareness can be had instantly. As soon as the mind carries on with its doubts, questions and tricks, notice that you are effortlessly aware of every thought. If you then just watch the thoughts from pure Awareness, without following a single one, they soon quieten down and give up. [2]

This is an ongoing process but it is no cause for despondency. For every time this occurs these negative thoughts can make you turn to Awareness itself and in Awareness there is only serenity and peace ... In fact, in the same way, every single thing in existence is a pointer towards Awareness. For everything perceived appears in this pure Awareness that you are.

This is easy to see by investigating the nature of one's moment-to-moment experience, and this book aims to provide a framework (see appendix) within which this investigation may be successfully carried out. This results in becoming 'aware of Awareness', after which one can carry out deeper investigations

---

[2] C. Drake, *Beyond The Separate Self,* 2009, Tomewin, p.36-37.

Awareness and Thought

into the nature of reality with this Awareness (of Awareness) as the starting point.

The great masters say that there is no end to Awakening and spiritual experience, there's always more to be found – what a wonderful idea! Sri Ramakrishna used to continually tell his devotees to 'go forward' and make further discoveries. You will find this is more than an idea, for you will discover that the deeper you go, the more you become 'aware of Awareness', the more that will be revealed.[3]

---

[3] C. Drake, *A Light Unto The Self,* 2011, Tomewin, p.97-101.

Chapter One

The Open Way

Details how Awakening by becoming aware of (and identifying with) Awareness is an 'open' way not requiring any special esoteric knowledge or practices.

I call Awakening by becoming aware of, and identifying with, Awareness 'The Open Way' because it is both 'open' and a 'way'. That is to say that it is not restricted, closed, covered or protected and is open to all people, situations and life-occurrences. It is also a way, a means, to Awaken and cultivation of this is a way, path, to full self--realization. Moreover, it is a way to be completely open to life with all of its possibilities and opportunities.

There are many other ways (means or paths) to Awakening but most require certain elements to be in place, thus restricting access to them. Typical elements are a guru, initiation, secret knowledge and practices, physical fitness, mental concentration and great discipline. Whereas becoming aware of, and identifying with, Awareness is very simple and open to all … see the appendix. The one element in common with all 'ways' is that they require great determination and persistence. For although 'the open way' is simple and the first Awakening occurs readily this is soon swamped by old thought patterns and samskaras (mental tendencies or 'well-worn grooves in the mind'). So Awakening needs to be established by repeated enquiry, or investigation, until one no longer 'nods off'.

This can take a long time, many life times some Buddhists say, but one need not be discouraged by this for every new Awakening fills one with a lightness of being as the worldly burdens are lifted, temporarily or permanently if slumber is not resumed. This lightness is so appealing that it makes enquiry/investigation a joy and thus persistence in this can be readily attained. So one need never say that one does not have time for, or is to busy to, enquire/investigate for this releases time by making us more alert and efficient. I recommend that one spend two or three periods of at least twenty minutes per day deeply relaxing into the recognition of Pure Awareness, as this will establish Awakening and make us less likely to be tossed by the storms of worldly life.

As being Awake is the means to overcome the mental suffering that is caused by identifying oneself as a separate object (in a universe of the same) then the occurrence of this can be recognised as a symptom that one has nodded off. So it can be used as a trigger to recommence investigation which can be performed in a few seconds by realizing that one is effortlessly aware of this mental suffering and (at the deepest level) one is this Awareness! In the same way if any remark causes offence, by taking it personally, then once again misidentification is occurring and so this can be used as another wake-up call. Thus the day is filled with multiple opportunities to reawaken and I am sure that you will discover many more …

The one thing that is required is the determination to Awaken and remain Awake whenever possible. This may sound onerous but the outcome of being Awake is so wonderful and freeing, compared to being trapped in a separate personal headspace, that this determination becomes self-nurturing requiring no effort. For when Awake one is open to all people, possibilities and situations. Once one sees that, at the deepest level, one is Pure Awareness, then one sees that 'others' are also That too, and this completely changes ones interaction with them. For they are then seen to be of the same essence, or essentially the same, as oneself and thus their needs and wishes become of equal weight to ones own! In fact one could go further and say that one sees all as oneself.

The 'all' that is mentioned does not only apply to people for, in the final analysis, all is consciousness existing in two modes – at rest as Pure Awareness and in motion as Cosmic Energy of which the universe(s) is a manifestation. Thus our body/minds are temporary manifestations of consciousness in motion, underlying which is Pure Awareness, consciousness at rest. So full Awakening produces this 'panoramic awareness' of no separation or nonduality. In this one is open to all possibilities and situations, as one is not restricted by protecting an imaginary separate personal self. Also one sees everything openly, as it actually is, and not covered or concealed by one's opinions, judgements, self-interest etc...

Chapter Two

Is Awareness The Absolute Reality?

Addresses the question of whether Awareness is the Absolute Reality and, regardless of the answer, whether there is anything that can be 'known' beyond this.

Is Awareness The Absolute Reality?

This is a question that is often considered and about which there are different views, but which is ultimately unanswerable. Anybody who claims to 'know' of a deeper level of the Absolute than Awareness is either following a belief or relying on an experience that underpins this 'knowing'. As these merely consist of thoughts, mental images, or sensations (ephemeral objects) which appear in (are 'seen by') Awareness, the constant conscious subjective presence, then they cannot be beyond Awareness. For if they could be then, by definition, we could not 'be aware' of them. Just as we cannot see anything that is beyond our field of vision, in the same way we cannot be aware of anything that is beyond (the field of) Awareness.

These beliefs and experiences puts this kind of 'knowing' into the same category as that of Hare-Krishna devotees who claim that Krishna is beyond Brahman (Pure Awareness). Once again any kind of vision or experience of Krishna appears in Awareness itself, or they could not be aware of it! Thus neither Krishna nor That, which some purport to be beyond Awareness, are actually proved to be so, for all of the evidence that their devotees can muster is just a collection of ephemeral objects appearing in Awareness itself … and thus obviously not beyond it.

That is not to say that either of these beliefs is necessarily incorrect, but we can have no way of knowing, as we would have to be aware of any 'way of knowing' (to say that it is correct) thus this (way of knowing) would appear in Awareness and thus, once again, not be beyond it …

It is fairly obvious that if there was a deeper level of the Absolute than Awareness we would, and could only, be unaware of it. There are some who say that Nirvikalpa Samadhi is totally beyond and in this state one is conscious of nothing, but this is actually "sthitha samadhi when the aspirant totally loses outer consciousness: he remains in this state for a long time, it may be many days"[4] which is actually no different from being unconscious ('not aware of, and responding to, one's environment' OED) and thus of no great value. It may result in a feeling of great peace when one comes out of it, but so does deep sleep until the mind grabs on to 'the story of me' as soon as it reactivates. In fact Ramakrishna, the great Indian Saint of the late nineteenth century, found that state so unsatisfying that he would sometimes bang himself on the top of the head when he would feel it coming on! About this he said: 'In [sthitha] samadhi one forgets the world. When the mind comes down a little I say to the Divine Mother "Mother please cure me of this"'[5]

Actually Nirvikalpa Samadhi is defined in Ramakrishna-Vedanta Wordbook as:

> The supreme transcendental state of consciousness in which the spiritual aspirant becomes completely absorbed in Brahman so all sense of duality is obliterated (p.52)

---

[4] M.Gupta, The Gospel of Ramakrishna,1942,Mylapore,p.702
[5] Ibid p.237

Is Awareness The Absolute Reality?

And further Brahman is defined in the Upanishads as:

> the agent by which the mind thinks, eye sees, tongue speaks, ear hears and body breathes (*Kena* I v.5-9). He is also described as the 'ear of the ear, eye of the eye, mind of the mind, word of the words and life of the life' (*Kena* I v.2). Thus He is the 'pure Awareness' (*Brihadaranyaka* 4 v.7) in which all thought, life and sensation appears; and He is the 'seer' (*Isha* v.8) and 'all knowing' (*Katha* 2 v.18). [6] He is also described as 'one' (*Isha* v.4), 'radiant, everywhere, transcendent, indivisible, pure' (v.8). As the cause, existence and dissolution of everything that exists, He is 'immortal, eternal, immutable' (*Katha* 2 v.18), 'without beginning or end, beyond time and space' (3 v.15), 'infinite, imperishable and unborn' (*Mundaka* II 1.1 & 1.2). Although He is 'within all' *(Isha* v.5) and 'the light of man' (*Brihadaranyaka* IV v.6) He is also 'unseeable, ineffable and unknowable' (*Kena* v.3). This is because He is 'pure consciousness' (*Aitareya* ch.3 v.1) and the 'attributeless reality' (*Svetasvetara* ch. 3 v.1). Thus all attributes appear in, exist in and disappear back into Brahman, but having no attributes He is unperceivable by the mind and the senses. Thus this 'pure Awareness', Brahman, is the substratum and essence of all of existence.[7]

---

[6] C. Drake, Humanity, *Our Place in The Universe*, 2010, Nonduality Books, Tomewin, p.50
[7] E. Easwaran, *The Upanishads*, 1988, Penguin, New Delhi

Is Awareness The Absolute Reality?

Therefore, according to the Upanishads, Brahman (The Absolute) is not beyond Awareness but is actually That. When one is totally identified with, and as, This then all sense of duality ceases and complete absorption in This is Nirvikalpa Samadhi. Beyond this state is what Sri Ramana Maharshi calls Sahaj Samadhi in which one is totally identified with (as) Awareness whilst living and operating in the manifest world.[8]

To posit that there is a deeper level than This is to argue for an improvable premise as we have seen. Even to say 'I intuit it' falls foul of the fact that we have to be aware of this to say it, and thus it is not beyond Awareness. So any discussion of, or belief in, this level deeper than Awareness is useless, and if followed is only itself an activity in Awareness. Moreover, it tends to make the 'believer' arrogant in the belief that he/she is in a very 'select group'. I recently had one of these tell me that I was only 'scratching at the surface' and that deeper 'knowing' was beyond me! If by this he means my mind is unable to 'know' anything beyond Awareness he's absolutely correct, what he fails to take into account is that the same applies to his mind!

Whereas, to discover Awareness of Awareness, and more than that the fact that at the deeper level we are this Awareness, see appendix, is child's play. When Awareness is investigated, honored, and identified with, this leads to peace, freedom, moksha, nirvana, call it what you will, which renders the search for any deeper level obsolete; especially

---

[8] A. Osborne, *Ramana Maharshi,* 1970, Weiser, Boston, p.45

Is Awareness The Absolute Reality?

as this is either unfounded or based on a belief, or experience, both of which are objects appearing in, and seen by Awareness itself.

The obvious fact is that we would and could, by definition, be unaware of any level deeper than Awareness itself, so any discussion about this is fruitless, and any conclusion about this is unknowable.

Chapter Three

Self-Referencing The 'Original Sin'

Discusses how 'self-referencing', that is how considering oneself as a separate object, and referring to oneself (mentally or verbally) as this, leads to unnecessary suffering.

Self-Referencing The 'Original Sin'

Here is an e-mail exchange I had with a reader of one of my books. I have re-ordered them so as to give the 'flow' of the exchange.

Hi Colin,

I've read almost your entire output of literature and even gave a 5-star critique to your writing. I have a full intellectual grasp of the principles of non-duality, and have studied the work of the great sages for several years. The problem, and it is quite severe, is that I am unable to apply this knowledge on an experiential level in my every day life. I would enjoy chatting with you by any means (Skype, email, telephone, etc.) in the hope that I can practically apply the knowledge I have gained over the years. At present, there remains substantial neurotic fear and identification with thought and the "small" self, while realizing my true nature seems elusive (even though it's always here!). Perhaps you could respond with some suggestions or guidance, both of which would be very welcome at this point.

Best Regards,

XXXX

Dear XXXX, In reply I would have to say just continue what you started when you wrote (earlier):

Self-Referencing The 'Original Sin'

> In particular, I've finally started to realize that periods of extreme emotional turmoil, which always seemed so debilitating and all-consuming, are nevertheless simply ephemeral thoughts and feelings which arise in this Awareness. They are seen to have no independent nature (or "power") independent of Awareness. This realization has been a great relief.

As you so correctly say it is a 'great relief' and if cultivated will completely solve your problem.... This may (will) take time to become completely established, as you know, but that is no reason to abandon the attempt. In fact now that you have tasted this 'relief' I doubt that you could abandon it! This is not an occupation for the dilettante, requiring total commitment, but the glimpses provide proof of the possible final outcome. Actually it requires one to be totally ruthless with the mind when it comes up with its old tricks to reassert control. As I have said before when it comes to identity *do not believe a single thought* but rely on experiential investigation. I suggest you use the procedure outlined in Investigation of Experience, chapter two of *Beyond,* every morning and evening, until some degree of establishment has occurred. I did this for ten years after I first developed it and still do occasionally...

Also the other practice (*Love Loving Itself* from *Awakening and Beyond*) I sent is very useful as it contains no reference to the small self and consists of consciousness using mind/body purely as an instrument ... which is all it is, nothing more!

Self-Referencing The 'Original Sin'

As Gangaji would say 'Buck Up!', even Papaji said he required to be vigilant with every breath, and Ramana said that self-realization is easy but after that the work starts! So let's keep working together whilst stopping to enjoy the view when the sacred glimpses occur, Love, Colin

The following day I added:

Dear XXXX, Although I completely stand by my earlier reply I realize that you were hoping for some new insight to help you deal with your 'problem'. This morning when I read 'self-grasping is to be totally forsaken' in my latest poem it crystallized something that I had been mulling over for some time. That is that even beyond self-grasping, which implies selfishness or compulsive thinking about oneself, self-referencing is the cause of most of our psychological problems. To highlight this here are two stanzas from different poems:

When we say 'I',
It's often a lie.
Denoting an apparently separate being,
From its looming extinction fleeing ...[9]

In fact we should studiously avoid,
Any thought which objectifies the 'I',
Which is pure Awareness and thus devoid,
Of characteristics ... the subjective 'eye'.[10]

---
[9] C. Drake, *Poetry From Beyond The Separate Self*, 2011, Tomewin, p.16.

[10] C. Drake, *Poetry From A Light Onto The Self*, 2012, Tomewin, p.58.

Self-Referencing The 'Original Sin'

For as soon as we use the word 'I' (or think it) most of us are immediately identifying ourselves as an object. Your comment "At present, there remains substantial neurotic fear and identification with thought and the 'small' self, while realizing my true nature seems elusive (even though it's always here!)" is a classic example. I know in my own case that as soon as I start judging, or evaluating, myself in any way this can cause mental suffering and is initiated by self-referencing. This is very insidious as most of us have been doing this all of our lives and we are encouraged to do so by western psychology, self help books, and even many 'spiritual paths'! Whereas, if this is abandoned, which it has to be for there is no separate 'I' (small self), then the problem vanishes.

There seem to me to be two ways to overcome this which need to go hand-in-hand. Firstly by continued investigation to discover that which is deeper than 'I", pure Awareness, which will lead to overcoming misidentification of ourselves as separate objects. Secondly by remaining vigilant (alert) to every occurrence of the word 'I' in our thoughts and evaluating these to see if they imply a separate object. If they do then instantly recognize that there is Awareness of this thought and you are this Awareness!

Self-Referencing The 'Original Sin'

Once one has reached the stage that these investigations into the thought 'I' reveal no misidentification, and thus cause no suffering, then there is no problem with using the term (I). For it is very difficult to operate in the world without this term, as you can see I use it a lot! But in the beginning one needs to be aware that its use can contains this insidious problem of self-referencing, and in most cases probably does! This seems to me to be the 'original sin' caused by (eating the apple of) discursive knowledge, that of separation, objectification, analysis and judging. However, if you realize that the term (I) is used in a purely conventional sense to denote the particular manifestation (and instrument) of Consciousness that is speaking (or thinking) then there is no problem. In fact this is Self-referencing, realizing the Self, which is the Totality of Being, consciousness at rest and in motion.

So it is very useful to investigate every use of the term 'I' to find out what this is implying. The key is that if this causes any mental suffering then self-referencing is occurring, and that investigation is needed to transform this into Self-referencing. After some time the latter will become second nature and the problem will no longer occur.

To wrap up the article here is my correspondent's reply:

Hi Colin,
Thanks for your concern. Actually, I'm doing beautifully since I

seriously started doing the "Love Loving Itself" exercise several times a day. I'm not certain precisely when a "shift" occurred, but my true nature as Awareness is now perceived with much greater clarity and consistency than the endless and unmerciful "story of Don". Ironically, this truth has been what I am since my very birth, right in front of my nose!

With Love and Thanks, XXXX

Chapter Four

Analysis The Disease Not The Cure

Posits that continual self-analysis (identified with, or as, the mind) perpetuates the dis-ease of misidentification.

Here is the continuing correspondence with XXXX from the previous article:

Hi Colin,

Thanks very much for all the timely assistance with my inquiries. As I practice and re-read "Beyond the Separate Self", I notice that my mind reacts by bringing up and spewing forth all sorts of issues and resistance to the realization of my true nature as Awareness. It's almost as if my mind has a "mind" of its own (sorry)! Is this typical and, if so, does the process eventually level off and become less noticeable. It seems as if my mind wants me to resolve so-called psychological issues from childhood such as abandonment, overindulgence, abuse, etc. Is it necessary to do all this, or should I just let the "dust" settle and continue the practice?
Many Thanks,
XXXX

Dear XXXX, I think that it is typical, and that is why I say that it requires one to be ruthless with one's mind. Do not suppress it or buy in to it just don't identify with it! I have never believed in western psychology's method of resolving childhood (or old) issues as this seems to me to be an endless process leading nowhere. If you believe in reincarnation (about which I have an open mind) then with most models one's intrinsic mind-stuff is carried over from past lives ... so how much regression work does this entail??!! No wonder psychiatrists (and past live therapists) have so much work! Once the mind is seen in its true context as a servant and not the master then all these old stories are seen just as entertainment, maybe not one's preferred choice but not as who one is. My next piece is going to be 'Analysis ... The Disease Not The Cure' which is a natural follow up to 'Self Referencing, The Original Sin'. So just don't give your mind (and its mind!) any weight by not letting it bother you, all of the rubbish it spews forth means **absolutely nothing** about 'who you are'! Love, Colin

P.S. The process will level off, but even if it doesn't so what! As long as you are not identifying with it then at the most it's just a b-grade movie, which may cause the occasional yawn but that's all...

The above is mainly concerned with psycho-analysis in which one attempts to resolve mental issues that occurred in one's early life and have lain semi-hidden in one's sub-conscious causing neurosis and anxiety. The problem with this approach is, as I have indicated above, it is almost endless and it gives the mind too much weight. In fact most psychiatrists would identify their patients with their minds and this assumption would naturally transfer to the patient ... if they hadn't already made this same assumption. So once again this perpetuates the misidentification of oneself as being a separate object, in a world of separate objects, which itself leads to neurosis and anxiety! So although the process may reduce these it can never overcome them and actually will subtly reinforce them. It is a case of 'pruning' (which actually encourages growth) rather than attacking the root of the problem, which is to be achieved by investigation of one's essential nature revealing that which one truly is – Pure Awareness. This discovery, when cultivated and established, destroys all existential anxiety and reduces neuroses to mere whimpers with no weight, like long lost hazy memories. Which is more than psycho-analysis is ever able to achieve…

Moreover, this is not the only form of analysis that is detrimental to Awakening, for many of us engage in semi-constant self-analysis with mental processes leading to conclusions such as:

> I wish I wasn't so selfish…
> I wish I could control my anger …
> I wish I was more intelligent …
> I wish I was more enlightened…
> I wish I was more Awake …
> I wish I could become more …
> If I do (or think) 'this' then 'that' will change …
> If only 'such and such' hadn't happened then things would be different …

> If 'they' hadn't done (or said) 'such and such' to me, then …
> I am so ….
> I am (anything that objectifies this 'I')
> Etc., Etc.,

It can be readily seen that this form of thinking generally presupposes that one is a separate object and is thus a form of misidentification, which will not help our anxiety but only increase it. In fact most of the people I know who indulge in this are depressed, which itself says something about the value of it (none!). Once again discovering the deeper level of Pure Awareness, which is our essential nature, is the antidote. This overcomes all desire to 'become' (something different) and all angst regards to the past or future, allowing us just to 'Be' in the Here and Now.

So in conclusion I regard analysis of one's self, or one's psyche, to be detrimental to Awakening as it strengthens the misidentification of oneself as a separate object. One of the cures being investigation (of experience, see appendix) to discover that which one truly 'is' Pure Awareness. Any other method that allows one to completely re-identify with 'The Totality of Being', or The Absolute, and overcome the above misidentification will do equally well.

Chapter Five

Oneness

Attempts to show, in a logical and scientific framework, that everything (or no-thing!) in existence is of the same essence – Consciousness.

Oneness

This article is designed to approach the subject of Oneness, the fact that everything (material or spiritual) is of the same essence, from a rational point of view. I will attempt to achieve this using the following framework:

1/ Modern physics has shown that all material is in fact energy, which implies (is synonymous with) motion. In fact atoms, whilst appearing to be a collection of 'things' (protons, neutrons, electrons etc...), have a wavelength which increases as they cool down (i.e. become slower) until finally at absolute zero they merge into a single 'matter field'. Therefore matter is just a complex series of vibrations, or movements.

2/ All motion originates from a field of stillness.

3/ All motion exists in a field of stillness.

4/ All motion is seen (there is Awareness of it) relative to this field of stillness.

5/ All motion finally returns to this field of stillness, when it runs out of energy.

The everyday example that I normally give is: if you walk across a room, before you start there is stillness, as you walk the room is still and you know you are moving relative to this stillness, and when you stop once again there is stillness.[11]

So let us consider theses elements in turn:

> 1/This manifestation of the universe occurred, according to modern science, as the 'big bang'. The universe (manifestation) expands, continually evolving and growing until the energy (matter) becomes so 'spread out' that it returns to the Oneness from whence it came. For energy is vibration (motion) and as the waves are stretched the peaks/troughs become smaller and smaller until all returns to stillness. To quote from a scientific paper on this, discussing what occurs as absolute zero is approached:[12]
>
>> Though individual atoms are typically thought as classical point particles with well defined positions and moments, the wave nature of matter becomes obvious at very low temperatures where the deBroglie wavelength associated with each atom is macroscopically large. When this becomes comparable to the inter atomic spacing then atoms lose their individuality, forming a Bose-Einstein-condensate (BEC). In this state a

---

[11] C. Drake, *Beyond The Separate Self*, 2009, Tomewin, p.43.
[12] C. Drake, *Awakening and Beyond*, 2012, Tomewin, p.134.

collection of millions of atoms can then be described as a single entity: a coherent matter field.[13]

Thus all matter will finally return to Oneness (a 'coherent matter field', in which no individuality, or 'thing', exists) and it will be a very cold universe as heat also implies movement, or energy, and in total stillness these are not present.

2/ It is an obvious fact that all motion is preceded by (and ends in) stillness. A common definition of motion is the movement from point A to point B, and these points are still.

3/ When motion occurs it is within a field of stillness. This field of stillness is saturated with Awareness at every level, from cells aware of and reacting to their environment, white blood corpuscles being aware of invading viruses, the mind being aware of thoughts/sensations, brainless moulds moving to the nearest food source that they are aware of etc., etc. It has also be demonstrated that even electrons change their behaviour when (aware of) being observed. In fact Awareness is the keystone, or substratum, of all life (and existence), without which it could not exist. This is also defined as consciousness at rest, aware of all movements that occur in it. To be totally

---

[13]http://www.deas.harvard.edu/haulab/publications/pdf/OPN_Ultraslow_light.pdf

aware of one's environment one needs to be still observing (and sensing) what is occurring.

4/ When motion occurs it is always known (there is Awareness of it) relative to a still point or to this field of stillness. For instance as a train pulls out of a station you know that it is moving by looking out of the window and seeing the still platform.

5/ All motion eventually returns to rest when it runs out of momentum, or energy. One of the 'holy grails' of scientists is to develop a 'perpetual motion' machine, but this has never been achieved, and can never be achieved without a continuous source of energy. Rather like the 'holy grail' of the alchemist to discover a substance that would turn lead into gold, another pipe dream!

So from Aware Nothingness (consciousness at rest) everything (all cosmic energy, consciousness in motion or motion in consciousness) exploded into being at the big bang, arising from the infinite potential energy already existing in this Aware Nothingness. This cosmic energy, manifesting as the universe, is continually evolving, rearranging and expanding at an ever increasing rate. As this occurs this will finally dissipate as each vibration finally 'runs out of steam' and returns to the stillness from whence it came. Thus all matter will finally return to nothingness (a 'coherent matter field', in which no individuality, or 'thing', exists) and it will indeed be a very cold universe as heat also implies movement, or energy, and in total stillness these are not present. However, this is no problem for Aware Nothingness (the coherent field), and does not imply that future universes could not come into being, issuing forth from this in the same way that ours did.[14] For as Aware Nothingness contains infinite potential energy that means that each point within it also contains that and so is a possible source of another 'big bang'.

Therefore, everything (material or spiritual) is of the same essence, that is to say consciousness (spirit), and so in reality there is only Oneness.

> Hail Pure Aware Nothingness,
>
> Consciousness at rest.
>
> In which nothing less,
>
> Than the totality is manifest.

---

[14] C. Drake, *Awakening and Beyond*, 2012, Tomewin, p.135.

Oneness

All things are cosmic energy,

Thus must be in motion,

Arising from the tranquility,

Of Consciousness, the ocean.

With no strain or effort,

Movements in stillness are projected,

And relative to this 'naught',

By Awareness they are detected.

Eventually they all peter out,

As they must run out of steam.

Back into stillness, without a doubt,

They subside, the end of a dream.

From Stillness all movements commence,

And in This Nothingness they also abide,

Relative to which This can them 'sense',

Back into Which they must subside.

Oneness

So all things come and go,

In Awareness, conscious and still.

As, and by, which we can know,

All of the things that this world fill.

Chapter Six

Loving 'What Is'

Addresses 'loving what is' - that is loving existence moment by moment as it actually 'is' and not as seen through by any filter of the mind, caused by ideology or misidentification.

Loving 'What Is'

A friend is always talking about 'Loving What Is' and it is something I can relate to. In an earlier essay I defined Love as 'No Separation', which implies that "Loving What Is' means "No Separation From What Is'. In absolute terms we are never separate from 'What Is' as there is only consciousness manifesting in many varied forms, thus everything (that Is) is of the same essence and so there is no separation. 'What Is' is defined as the manifestation (of Consciousness) ***as it actually is*** and not as overlaid with any ideology or personal 'story'.

However, to exhibit, and feel, this love one needs to feel no separation, that is to say that one needs to be identified as (a manifestation of) Consciousness itself. Now Consciousness has two 'modes' - at rest as Pure Awareness and in motion as cosmic energy, the manifest universe. So if one can discover that at the deepest level one is the constant conscious subjective presence, Pure Awareness, negotiating the physical world in a particular manifestation of cosmic energy (this human body) then this correct identification has occurred. This is extremely simple to do, see appendix, by investigating the nature of our moment to moment experience.

Moreover, any objective label we apply to ourselves which implies separation, or identification of ourselves as a distinct object, will impede the above process and result in us feeling separate from 'What Is' and thus losing this 'loving feeling'. Now my friend is really into astrology, which many people use to define themselves and those around them, in which case it labels us in the way just considered. His response was that astrology is part of 'What Is' and thus one can love that too. I have no problem with this or any other system of classification if they are held in context as just entertainment, or ways of defining personality types, whilst being aware that what they are labeling is just the ephemeral manifestation (body/mind) and not the essence of what one is. However, astrology falls foul of the definition of 'What Is' being an ideology, that is to say that it is a framework through which the world (and especially humanity) is perceived.

The danger is that people tend to identify with these labels and each adds another level of misidentification which needs to be stripped away to discover our essential being and realize 'No Separation from What Is'. Another danger is that if one accepts that all human ideologies are part of 'What Is' and can thus be loved then this means that Nazism, Sadism, Masochism, Racism, etc. also fall into this category … Whereas, these are actually all ways of viewing the world which prevents one from experiencing 'What Is'. Actually one only truly experiences 'What Is' when the mind is still and is not judging, comparing, analyzing or seeing through any previous framework of reference.

> How freeing to see with a clear mind,
> No concepts or labels to obscure the view,
> Once our true identity we find,
> Pure Awareness, when we see the world anew!

Loving 'What Is'

So if you identify with any ideology, or objective label, and see the world from this point of view you stop seeing it as it truly Is. In which case one is unable to Love 'What Is'.

There are many things that we are told,
Have meaning as to who, or what, we are,
Our body whether young or old,
Possessions, maybe even our fancy car!

Our occupation and astrology,
'Chinese year' and nationality.
Our religion and numerology,
Ancestry and personality.

It's true they influence the body/mind,
With which if we misidentify,
Makes it more difficult to find,
Awareness our true identity,

For each adds another layer,
Of separation and partition,
Which must be peeled away ere,
We Awaken, thus completing our 'mission'.

Loving 'What Is'

So we must be careful not to read,
Meaning into things which come and go,
Thoughts and sensations which are the seed,
When clung to as 'ourselves', the ego.

At the deepest, fundamental level,
No things have essential meaning,
If not seen this our lives bedevil,
Clouding existence with its gleaning.[15]

All is Consciousness, at rest or at play,
The former Awareness, the unmanifest,
And creation, cosmic energy that may,
Be 'seen' in motion, ere returning to rest.

When Awake 'we' can truly play the game,
With no-self we joyfully participate.
When 'asleep' we cannot do the same,
Identified as an object that is separate.

When the world is met with a still mind,
With no reference to an individual seer,

---

[15] C. Drake, *Poetry From A Light Onto The Self*, 2012, Tomewin, p.56-58.

Its wonder and beauty we can find,
Needing no extra purpose for us to cheer.

As an instrument of Consciousness can
Creation experience and enjoy,
Mind/body is more useful than
A discrete object, or a cosmic toy.

All conscious beings fulfill this function,
Through which Awareness can participate,
And spontaneously live with no compunction,
Allowing Consciousness to Itself relate.

Amazement, awe and gratitude,
Are outcomes of seeing the world this way,
As Awareness without personal attitude,
There is no separation from the play.

It is only when identified with body or mind,
As a unique, separate human being,
Extra purpose or meaning we need to find,
For existence 'as it is' we are not seeing.[16]

---

[16] C. Drake, *Poetry From A Light Onto The Self*, 2012, Tomewin, p.50-52.

This article produced some interesting responses. One from my friend who phoned to say that he isn't 'really into astrology' and another from a lady who is and was somewhat incensed that I should denigrate it. What she appeared to overlook was that I was not saying anything about (the validity of) astrology per se, but was just using it as an example of an ideology (or way of looking at the world) which could prevent one from 'Loving What Is'. However, to be fair to her she did say that *everything that one clings to with any identification is a misrepresentation of Self* which showed clear understanding.

Chapter Seven

Ego Is Misidentification

Discusses ego and shows how, by considering its various definitions, it is synonymous with misidentifying oneself as a separate object (in a universe of such).

Ego Is Misidentification

I recently received the following in reply to chapter three *Self-Referencing the 'Original Sin'*:

> While I agree with your advice for twenty-first century humans, I don't see self-referencing as 'original sin' or the 'fall of man' either; in my opinion, based on ancient doctrines, self-referencing or development of ego was actually a significant evolutionary advance for man on this earth, many millenia ago, a product of the help of many advanced intelligences, that took him out of total imbeddedness in nature with no insight into what he was. He became individualized instead of one of the herd, so to speak, and then began an upward course. Too many teachings think he fell from grace or somehow forgot who he was, or that mysteriously the One forgot what it was, or apparently forgot, whatever, etc... But is it really so? I don't see separation as a mistake, but as part of the plan... 'That's how Pop (er, the One) wanted it," as Michael Corleone might have said to Fredo. In this sense I agree with Anadi, that the ego is really quite an advanced state: the first 'initiation', one might say.

Now in the original article I said: "This seems to me to be the 'original sin' caused by (eating the apple of) discursive knowledge, that of separation, objectification, analysis and judging" which is borne out by the biblical account in Genesis chapter three. The story goes that Eve, urged on by a snake, ate the fruit of the 'tree of knowledge' and shared this with Adam. After this they realized that they were naked and covered themselves with leaves when Jehovah appeared. When he asked them why they did this they said they were afraid to appear naked before Him, and as they have never done this before He immediately realized what they had done. He was so angry that he cursed them with suffering and cast them out of the garden.

For, before the eating of the apple Adam and Eve had no self-image (ego) and thus were unworried by being naked. However, after the snack they realised that they were naked (by discursive knowledge, that of separation, objectification, analysis and judging) and this became a cause of shame (or negative self-image) thus they made clothes to cover themselves. This self-image of a separate objective being, that was naked and thus separate from other beings and from the source of being (God, Consciousness), is the cause of all of humanity's consequent ills …

The term 'original sin' is a Christian one relating to this story which I think makes a good point if taken as a metaphor and not the literal truth. So I can hardly agree with my correspondent's statement: 'based on ancient doctrines, self-referencing or development of ego was actually a significant evolutionary advance for man on this earth'. This is not to say that I am against all 'discursive knowledge, that of separation, objectification, analysis and judging' which is very useful for negotiating and examining the physical world, but is a disaster when applied to identifying what in essence we truly 'are'.

As far as the ego being an 'advanced state' is concerned, what exactly is being posited here? To examine this and whether the ego actually even exists we need to define the beast itself. The following definitions are given in the Oxford English Dictionary:

> 1/ A person's sense of self-esteem or self-importance.
>
> 2/ *Psychoanalysis* The part of the mind that mediates between the conscious and the unconscious and is responsible for reality testing and a sense of personal identity.
>
> 3/ *Metaphysics* A conscious thinking subject.

So let us consider these in turn:

> 1/ "A person's sense of self-esteem or self-importance." Which is obviously only a subjective opinion based on the assumption that one is a separate person, or self. That is not to say that self-esteem is not very useful in negotiating the physical world but it is always fragile when one is identified as a person, or the small self. However, if one is identified as being a manifestation (and instrument) of Consciousness (or Awareness), and one consequently identifies all others as That, then this leads to an unshakeable Self-esteem which is even more useful than the limited version based on misidentification.

2/ "*Psychoanalysis* The part of the mind that mediates between the conscious and the unconscious and is responsible for reality testing and a sense of personal identity."

This assumes that the mind is an objective thing, as only a thing can have parts, which disagrees with its definition as 'the faculty of consciousness or thought' (OED). In fact the mind is just experienced as a flow of thoughts and mental images. But even more to the point is that it is responsible for 'a sense of personal identity' and thus the source of misidentification

3/ "*Metaphysics* A conscious thinking subject." This is getting close to the reality of our essence as 'the constant conscious subjective presence' which is Pure Awareness. However the definition still implies a separate object rather than a shared presence and so is still a cause of misidentification.

So based on all of the above, I would have to disagree that the ego is 'an advanced state' and would even go so far as to say that it is synonymous with identifying as a separate object and so **is** misidentification itself. When one overcomes this by discovering that one is actually just Pure Awareness, which is easy to do by investigation of one's immediate experience (see appendix), then the ego is seen for what it is - just a fake masquerading for what (or who) we actually are.

Chapter Eight

The Myth of Ego

Continues the theme of the previous chapter to show that ego is actually a mythical entity. It also highlights the differences between ego and character, or personality, and posits that these two are necessary whereas the former is illusory.

Lately I have become aware of how entrenched is the myth of ego - that it exists, is necessary for day to day living, is useful, or is an 'advanced state'. In discussions with many friends on the spiritual path I have realized how pervasive these ideas are and how difficult they are to overcome. In fact I used to say that the ego was useful as long as one doesn't identify with it ... The problem with all of this is that it confuses 'character' (or personality) with ego, which I defined in the previous chapter as being synonymous with misidentification of oneself as a separate object in a universe of separate objects. Not only does this cause feelings of separation and suffering but it makes us view 'others' in this light and treat them as objects also ... which leads to selfishness and exploitation (of 'others') with all of its many negative outcomes.

That is not to say that we are not all unique manifestations of Consciousness (Awareness when at rest and Cosmic Energy when in motion) and appear to be separate at the level of body/mind. But this is just an appearance, as at the deepest level we are all of the same essence - Consciousness itself, of which body/mind is an instrument through which That can experience engage with and enjoy its manifestation, the physical world. Total identification with This leads to seeing all 'others' as That also and treating them as essentially the same as oneself.

To live in a useful and harmonious way one does indeed need character, defined in the OED as: 'mental and moral qualities' and 'strength and originality'. Also one will naturally have a personality defined as: 'the combination of characteristics and qualities that form an individual's distinctive character'. But one needs to realize that this individuality is confined to the body/mind and not the essence (Consciousness) of which body/mind is an ephemeral manifestation. Thus character and personality are necessary traits for living in the world, but the same is not true of ego which is actually a mythical entity synonymous with misidentification.

This may sound like splitting hairs but it is actually of vital importance for one cannot possibly go 'beyond the separate self' and identify with the universal essence (Consciousness, Awareness) whilst egoically clinging to the small self - identifying oneself as a separate object. This leads to self-importance, self-grasping, self-referencing, self-nurturing, self-analysis, self-loathing, and all of the other ills attributed to the small self. Whereas discovering one's true identity as Awareness (see appendix), which is the true Self, leads to Self-esteem, Self-inclusiveness, Self-love, etc. That is loving and esteeming the Self which includes all, identification with which leads to a life without angst and mental suffering.

With this outlook one can quite happily think of oneself as a wonderful, unique manifestation of the universal essence (Consciousness, Awareness) which does not lead to self-grasping as within this there is actually no separate self. Thus it does not lead to feelings of separation from (and exploitation of) 'others' as they too are seen as unique manifestations of the same essence. This form of Self-esteem (as opposed to self-esteem) gives one confidence in day to day living and is totally unshakeable as long as one stays identified with the true Self - Consciousness, Awareness when at rest and Cosmic Energy (The Manifest Universe) when in motion.

Chapter Nine

Why Write About The Ineffable?

This chapter was prompted by people questioning my motives for writing on the subject of Awakening and Awareness. It also came about when a friend posited that it's pointless attempting to put the ineffable into words.

Why Write About The Ineffable?

At a recent meeting of our weekly coffee/philosophical discussion group somebody kept asking the question: 'why does anybody write about Reality/The Truth/Nonduality etc., when it cannot be put into words and anything that is said about it actually subtly misrepresents it?' I have also been asked many times why do I write on this subject especially as we all know that the 'The Tao that can be spoken is not the Tao' (Tao Te Ching verse 1).

As many people have misguided views on the subject of the motivations of writers of spiritual books I decided to try to 'put the record straight'. Firstly I will consider these various views and attempt to clarify them from my point of view. There are basically three cynical opinions:

1/ We do it for the money. In fact everything I write is disseminated freely to my e-mail group (which all are welcome to join by contacting me at colin108@dodo.com.au) before becoming part of a book. Now I know that there are a few authors, Deepak Chopra and Eckhart Tolle spring to mind, who sell vast numbers of books, but I imagine that my experience is more typical. Over the last three years since *Beyond The Separate Self,* and the following five books, have been published I have sold about 750 books in total. After taking editing, advertising and indexing into account there is barely enough left for Janet and I to pay for our weekly coffee!

Why Write About The Ineffable?

2/ We do it to get famous. At this level the aim of the game is to recognize that no separate individual self (person) exists, and to realize that at the deepest level there is only pure Awareness or consciousness of which every thing in existence is an ephemeral manifestation. So who (or what) is there to get famous? Even if apparent fame occurs so what? It's just another temporary happening of no consequence in the cosmic scheme of things …

At a more mundane level, if getting well known means that my 'pointings' reach more people then it's all to the good. I have no intention, however, of travelling the world holding meetings to enable this. I attempt to write in such a clear manner that my message is transparent, and the fact that I get so few questions from readers of my books tends to attest to this.

3/ We do it for the power. Somebody recently said to me that I had a 'Messiah Complex' to which I replied: "It's not that. We just all do the best we can to Awaken and help each other along the way".

This just about sums it up for me; having discovered the absolute ease of Awakening through investigating the nature of our moment-to-moment experience (see the appendix) and seeing the needless unnecessary suffering around me I have no alternative but to share what I can. If I degrade the pure nature of The Tao, The Absolute, Brahman … call it what you will, by doing this then so be it. In fact this

Why Write About The Ineffable?

Absolute can only be discovered experientially for oneself and others can only act as pointers along the way.

If all Awakened beings (or their followers) had decided there was no point in writing, or talking, about this subject then there would be no scriptures, religions, mystical paths, spiritual books, practices, rituals, satsangs, retreats etc.... Just a few silent enlightened beings with the remainder of the population unaware of the fact that Awakening was even possible!

I would like to share a response I received to one of the 'offerings' I sent to my e-mail group:

Dear Colin

Thanks so very much for your writings
Of late I have been bombarded with experiences that keep drawing me out of Awareness. Your email and its links have bought me back to Awareness and restoration of hope and stillness. That is priceless!!!! I was at my wits end and desperate yet as always I had forgotten and Awareness was and always is still and there. My life was saved because your musings reminded me that Awareness is always there. Thankyou

Yours in Truth, XXXX

As I am sure you can all imagine, such affirmation as to the usefulness of writing about Awareness is worth a lot more than any amount of money, fame or power. For as the Dalai Lama said:

Why Write About The Ineffable?

> From my own limited experience I have found that the greatest degree of inner tranquility comes from the development of love and compassion. The more we care for the happiness of others, the greater our own sense of well-being becomes... It is the ultimate source of success in life. [17]

Naturally, being human (at the surface level), I have more 'selfish' reasons for writing on this subject:

1/ As a way of staying Awake, for when one is contemplating and writing about Awareness this keeps one 'aware of Awareness' and thus Awake.

2/ For the pure joy of doing so, for being Awake is naturally joyful and carefree, so that any activity which fosters Awakening will lead to joy.

3/ As a way of clarifying my 'understanding' and putting into words my 'discoveries' from my periods of meditation and contemplation.

As time goes by you will make your own discoveries and verbalize your own pathways into this recognition. I strongly advise you to record in writing these discoveries and pathways, as the reading of them before your practice will put you in the right frame of mind, and inspire you. In the final analysis your 'pathway in' will become particular to your own mind, and writings produced by your mind will always appeal more than those produced by another mind. Ultimately you have to become, as the Buddha said, 'a light unto yourself'[18].

In fact if my e-mails stimulate this process and remind you that Awareness is always present (and at the deepest level that is what you

---

[17] C. Drake, *Humanity, Our Place in The Universe,* 2010, Tomewin, p.71
[18] C. Drake, *Beyond the Separate Self,* 2009, Tomewin, p.91

Why Write About The Ineffable?

are!) then they will have done their job. Whether you read them or not is totally irrelevant if just seeing the name of the sender can bring you back to an instant recognition (or remembrance) of That which you are: Pure Awareness.

Chapter Ten

The 'Problem' of Negative Thoughts

This is my response to the question of why the majority of thoughts appear to be negative.

The 'Problem' of Negative Thoughts

Here is an e-mail I received on the subject of negative thoughts:

Thank you Colin. Hope you had a wonderful trip. In addition to the previous question, I have another question I hope you don't mind answering.

If mind/thoughts are ephemeral objects, why does it appear that the ones that are arising at the mind/body level are always "negative"? Within the stillness of awareness, it appears one has to be on "guard" to ignore these particular thoughts. But why do they arise in the first place versus "good/positive" thoughts?

Here is my reply:

It is not my experience (luckily) that thoughts at the mind/body level are always negative. In fact my level of enjoyment of the natural world through the senses engenders many positive thoughts of joy, bliss, ecstasy etc ... Also I am very fortunate to be blessed with a mind that always looks for the silver-lining (or positive) in any given situation. I suspect that one can foster this by practice, whenever any apparently negative situation arises just examine it objectively and see whether it has any positive elements. If so, then value these more highly than the seemingly negative ones.

The 'Problem' of Negative Thoughts

However, I do get what you are asking and I suspect that it is tied up with the main function of the mind as a problem-solving device, one's on-board computer. For positive thoughts do not present any problem and are thus not grist to the mill of a problem-solver. Whereas negative thoughts often present (apparent) problems that need to be addressed and in this way can be very useful.

For example, say you are planning an outdoor party. Now the positive (optimistic) mind will say that the weather will be fine so no need to worry. On the other hand, the negative (pessimistic) mind will say that it will probably rain and this will ruin the event. This, however, gives an opportunity for the mind to do its thing and plan for rain by producing a plan B. So the optimistic mind full of positive thoughts will be undone by the bad weather whereas the pessimistic mind full of negative thoughts will have the problem covered.

The problem is that the mind is continually searching for problems to solve and if none are present it will either needlessly speculate about the future or wallow in the past looking for the causes of our present problems hoping by this to understand and solve them. If this doesn't produce any problem-solving work it will consider the present in a negative light to see if it can't come up with a problem to solve!

However, none of this is a problem if one is not identified with the mind but with the Pure Awareness in which it appears. In this case the mind will slowly settle as it runs out of problems to solve and is put into its place as a servant (or instrument) and not the master (or the essence). Whereas, if one is identified as the mind then even the (non-existent) problem of negative thoughts just gives it more fuel to run on!

To see more on this subject please re-read chapter one of *Beyond The Separate Self* which is aptly titled 'The Problem'!

Hope this is of some help and not a problem ... Love, Colin

To complete this article here is the reply to this and the following chapter:

Good Morning Colin,

Wow! What a good morning to open my mailbox and see the wonderful response from you. Chapter 13: Nothing to Do, No Problem to Solve (Beyond the Separate Self) is being read and Chapter 1 will be re-read. In essence, there is no such thing as a negative thoughts, just the mind seeking an alternative way or action on how to survive or solve a particular situation or problem (even if it doesn't exist). Again, your clarity and insight are a blessing to all coming into contact with your work. Thank you!!!

Love, XXXX

Chapter Eleven

Handling Prejudice, Worldly and Racial

This is my response to the same questioner, as the previous chapter, who 'suffers' from worldly and racial prejudice and was asking how this could be addressed.

Here is the first question put by my reader from the previous chapter:

Dear Colin,

This essence manifested itself in the body form with dark skin. In striving to live in pure awareness daily, how does one deal with prejudices of skin color and non-religious living bias while trying not to be judgmental towards others whose actions cause harm to spirit, mind, and body?

Again, thank you in advance for your response.

Here is my response:

The vast majority of people are asleep, thus spiritually ignorant, and of these most are not seriously interested in Awakening. So one needs to be careful about discussing this topic, or any related topic, with these. It is best not to bring the subject up unless there seems to be an interest in it. Interestingly, I have discovered that nearly everyone has some interest in it when it is discussed on a one-to-one basis and if it just comes up without being obviously introduced into the conversation. So when talking with another it is good to stay alert to this possibility.

As far as harm is concerned, if there is bodily danger it is obviously best to negate this by defending oneself or absconding ... The spirit, Pure Awareness, is impervious to harm and thus there is no need to worry about This. The mind will only suffer if one identifies with it ... If it is regarded purely as an instrument then it will not hold onto seemingly hurtful remarks as it does not take them personally. In fact this is the key, for when one is identified as Pure Awareness then one does not take anything personally ... as one realizes that one is not a person! On the Bodhisattva Path there is a stage at which one does not even take physical assault personally:

> The third stage is called the 'luminous' in which one develops *patience* and forbearance thus overcoming anger. Once again selflessness is the key: 'Furthermore for the bodhisattva who has seen selflessness, what is cut [i.e. his body] by whom, at what time and in what manner - all these phenomena are seen to be like reflections. Therefore he is patient' (3.2).[19] To generate anger one must identify with a 'self' that is under attack, either physically or mentally, whereas a bodhisattva has compassion for the bad karma created for and by the attacker. This ground is called 'luminous' for through the knowledge of no self, and thus emptiness, one experiences a luminous glow that pervades the whole environment on arising from meditation.

---

[19] This quote comes from the 'Guide to the Middle Way' by Chandrakirti, the principal disciple of Nagarjuna, which is contained in: G. K. Gyatso, *Ocean of Nectar*, 1995, London

Handling Prejudice, Worldly and Racial

I realize this may all sound somewhat theoretical but you will find that the more identified you become with Pure Awareness the more it becomes your direct experience. Consider the following questions and answers from Awakening and Beyond: [20]

> **Is it possible to live so maturely from the ego that it looks like Awakening?**
>
> No, for the ego will always take itself seriously and defend itself when under attack.
>
> **Conversely, is there a life of Awakening that looks wild, untamed, and immature?**
>
> Possibly, all models and personalities differ.
>
> **How can someone know the difference?**
>
> If the person in question never takes offence, thus has no self-image, then they are Awake.

With regard to racial prejudice, this is obviously due to ignorance and bigotry and should not be taken seriously. Sure, you may argue, but it is painful ... However, once again as you stop taking it personally it

---

[20] C. Drake, *Awakening and Beyond*, 2012, Tomewin, p.125.

will lose its bite. As far as it affecting one's worldly prospects are concerned I'm afraid the world is not a fair place, and as one Awakens these lose their seeming extreme importance. I suffered from a limited version of this, class prejudice, when I spent seven years in an English 'Public School' (the domain of the middle and upper classes) having come from a lower working class background. In this environment bullying was rife and I soon learned to either keep my head down or defend myself when appropriate. Also I was never considered for any leadership role as I was just a pleb!

As far as judging one's persecutors goes, this will lessen as you Awaken for you will start to see that they are of the same essence as yourself and their behavior is caused by ignorance… you will even begin to develop compassion for their condition! But do not be too hard on yourself if this takes some time to manifest, as the habit to judge others can be very deeply ingrained. You could always adopt Swami Vivekananda's[21] approach ... when he was asked how to deal with people who ridiculed his spiritual beliefs and lifestyle he said he would give their opinions no more weight than those of dogs yapping at his heels! That is not to say that one should regard them as dogs, just their opinions … which is not demeaning for you should not demean yourself by identifying with your mind and likewise you should not demean 'others' by identifying them with their minds (opinions).

I do hope this has been of some help, Love, Colin

---

[21] Sri Ramakrishna's main disciple who bought Vedanta to the US in the late 1890s.

Chapter Twelve

Awakening By Becoming Aware of Awareness

This is a hundred line poem dealing with overcoming mental suffering and misidentification by becoming aware of Awareness, the constant conscious subjective presence, and identifying with (and as) this.

Awakening by Becoming Aware of Awareness

In an early *Sutta* Buddha is said to comment:
'Awareness of Awareness, investigation of the way,
Are the first two factors of enlightenment'.
By examining our nature, discover these we may…

For this to be really so
The starting point is a naked mind.
All 'knowing' one must let go,
So we don't 'clothe' that which we find.

Although all dogma must be abhorred,
There are mystical paths we can follow.
Such pointers need not be ignored,
But abandoned if found to be hollow.

Finally one must discover the truth for oneself,
Seeing clearly throughout the investigation,
For this, beliefs should be left on the shelf,
Then what's found suffers no degradation.

So the discoveries that we may make,
Our direct experience they will be,
When aware of Awareness, thus Awake,
Requiring no outside authority.

If we identify as a separate being
In a hostile universe,
Then we have no choice but seeing
Manifestation as diverse.

When we think of ourselves as an object
And others that as well,
An imaginary self-image we project,
Which can create a living hell.

From this mind-created suffering ensues.
Not mental or physical pain,
But the outcome of the mind which 'stews'
On these, as they wax and wane.

Of status, position, achievements, occupation,
Our individual self-image is made,
Mental prowess, appearance, family situation,
Future goals and memories that fade.

Identification with this will presage
Insecurity, angst and fear.
Postponed by bolstering this image,
Searching for 'more' to appear.

Making us live in the past or future,
Not seeing things as they 'are'.
The eternal now we cannot nurture,
And this does each moment mar.

Self-image is an imaginary construct,
Absent, there's no fear of losing face,
With no-self there is nothing to protect.
This realization needs to take place.

Awakening by Becoming Aware of Awareness

To Awaken, rouse yourself from this dream,

Of being a separate object on the earth.

No matter how bewitching this may seem,

An illusion society has fostered since your birth

To see this, into your own nature enquire,

To discover the underlying strata,

Where thoughts and feelings rise, then expire.

The perceiver of this ephemeral data.

The body is experienced as a flow of sensations,

The mind as a flow of images and thought.

What is it, then, that notices these presentations?

The constant subject that need never be sought.

That which we feel we have always been,

The unchanging basis of this very life,

That which all of our moments has seen,

Our ups and downs, joys, struggles and strife.

Awakening by Becoming Aware of Awareness

The clue is that, to live, aware we must be

Of mind and body, from head to toe;

So Awareness, itself, is That which these see.

The changeless that doesn't come and go.

Check it out in this moment, now

Notice how thoughts and sensations to and fro,

In ever present Awareness, that is how

Our experiences we can enjoy and know.

So This is what we are, have always been.

Wake up to this fact, by truly knowing

That, which our whole life-story has seen.

A constant witnessing presence, no thing!

From birth to death life is a continual series

Of thoughts, sensations and mental images,

Which are our moment to moment experiences.

And That which sees these in all of their stages.

Awakening by Becoming Aware of Awareness

A torrent of objects that arrive and depart

In this conscious perceiving presence,

Awareness, the fundamental heart,

Neath body and mind, our ultimate essence.

Awareness is universal consciousness at rest,

Within which all things come and go,

As motion, in consciousness, is the manifest*

And in stillness all movements ebb and flow.

Awareness is ever silent and still

Omniscient and omnipresent,

Witnessing all vibrations that mill…

That from which all things are 'lent'.

In which they are perceived and reside,

Pure and pristine, by things unaffected,

Omnipotent for into This they subside.

By whose radiance they are detected.

Thus the properties of Awareness that we have found

Agree with those, of the Absolute, religions posit

Without the Person those 'of the Book' propound

However, all persons are manifestations of It!

* Cosmic energy for energy implies (is synonymous with) motion. Modern physics has shown that all matter is comprised of energy and is thus just a complex series of movements, or vibrations.

Chapter 13

Simplicity and Complexity

Discusses the absolute simplicity of this method of Awakening and compares this with the many complex systems, ideologies and categories of (mis) identification which seem to appeal to the human mind.

Simplicity and Complexity

We have already discovered the absolute simplicity of Awakening by becoming aware of Awareness and then identifying with this, the deeper level of being in which all thoughts, mental images and sensations are seen (see appendix). Moreover, this is consciousness at rest in which all things (forms of cosmic energy, consciousness in motion) arise, abide and finally subside. However, this absolute simplicity does not appeal to the human mind which loves complexity, categorization, compartmentalization, labelling and conceptualization.

This is especially so in the area of identification, that is in defining what we actually are, and also in spirituality in general. There are various categories that are used in this process that can be seen to include most forms of misidentification – labeling us as being separate objects (in a universe of the same) or as members of an elite group, many of which claim to have comparatively deeper understanding of the truth of reality. Some of these categories are:

The 'Ism(s)' – *Unspecified system, philosophy or ideological movement (OED).*
Examples being: Buddhism, Hinduism, Islamism, Judaism, Vashnavism, Saivism etc ...
There are also more worldly examples e.g. communism, masochism, sadism, pacifism etc ...

The Olog(ies) – *A subject of study or interest (OED).*

Examples being: Numerology, astrology, psychology, scientology, phrenology, ideology etc...

These are considered by their devotees to be more than just interests but to actually help in defining what one is, one's actual identity.

There are again more worldly examples such as morphology, radiology, chronology etc ...

The Ian(s) - *Suffixes which form adjectives or nouns (OED)* normally used in labeling.

Examples being: Christian, Australian, Siberian, Canadian, Austrian, Indonesian, etc ...

A simpler version of this is 'an' e.g. American, German, Mexican etc ...

Note that these also purport to say something about what we actually are. It is interesting to note that these form the noun by adding the indefinite article 'an' to the end, also implying a separate object ...

The It(ies) - *Suffixes which form nouns denoting quality or condition (OED)*

Such as: Christianity, Divinity, Spirituality, Catholicity, Nationality, Personality etc ...

Needless to say there are many more worldly examples, but the ones given above tend to denote categories that we are associated with and say something about our identity. They even form the noun by adding 'it' which itself denotes a separate object!

This is not to say that some members of these categories do not have pointers to our true identity embedded within them, especially the religions, but they have overlaid this with so much dogma and complication that it is very difficult to unearth. So I would advise any one of you that has directly discovered that one is, at the deepest level, Pure Awareness to treat them all with kid gloves.

Especially dangerous are the tendencies to feel that one belongs to any category, as this can lead to a subtle (or not so subtle) form of tribalism, and any description of oneself that the 'system' imposes which defines one as a separate individual object. Rumi was aware of the danger of this as Coleman Barks points out:

> And he made it clear that someone who considers nation or religion an important human category is in danger from severing the heart from its ability to act compassionately. This is a radical idea now, but Rumi held this conviction in the thirteenth century with such deep gentleness that its truth was recognized.[22]

---

[22] Barks C. *The Essential* Rumi, 1995, London, P.246

For the problem is that if you identify as belonging to any particular group you will tend to favor other members of this group and could discriminate against those who are non-members. Also if you identify as a separate individual object you will identify others as that and thus be liable to treat them as objects. Whereas true compassion stems from 'seeing all as oneself', that is identifying all as being of the same essence and thus essentially the same as oneself.

In fact it is best to steer clear of them all by avoiding any labeling of oneself in any way that could lead to this erroneous conclusion. The continued investigation of, relaxation into and identification with Pure Awareness is the key to achieve this. This is the simplest way to discover the true nature of self-identity without having to fight through the morass of complexity imposed by the various systems categorized above. It also conforms to Ockham's Razor given colloquially as 'the simplest solution is the best' and defined in the OED as 'the scientific principle that in explaining a thing no more assumptions should be made than are necessary'.

For, in the investigation of one's moment to moment experience (see appendix) which reveals that at the deepest level one is Pure Awareness, no assumptions need to be made or relied upon. And this also provides the simplest explanation of self-identity requiring no beliefs, just that which is directly discovered ...

Chapter 14

The Miraculous and The Auspicious

Considers humanity's fascination with the so-called miraculous and auspicious. It attempts to show that every moment is auspicious for Awakening and, once Awake, then everything is seen to be miraculous.

The Miraculous and The Auspicious

Recently I was at a kirtan (chant) held to celebrate the ending of the Mayan Calendar cycle and the summer (winter for most of you) solstice. Before the chanting people were asked to comment and there were some interesting things said:

> One was about a previous gathering on an auspicious 11/11 (I can't remember the year) to celebrate this. 11/11 is meant to be very significant:
>> *The 11:11 is the bridge to an entirely different spiral or energy patterning. It is the step beyond the known dimensional universe into a new patterning of Octaves.*
>
> It was said that miraculous things happened at this gathering.

The second was about a well known guru who is purported to have said, back in the early 1970s, that the 21st of December 2012 was an especially auspicious day when people would have the possibility to readily go beyond their karma by letting go of the past and embarking on spiritual renewal.

The third was that this was a day when one should avail oneself of this opportunity to enter the fifth dimension (?) or one would be stuck in the day to day four dimensional model. Presumably this means that 'Awakening' was readily available on that day but would be more difficult if one 'missed the boat'

The Miraculous and The Auspicious

All of which made me ponder humanity's obsession with 'auspicious days' and the miraculous. Now I like a good party (especially combined with chanting) as much as anyone (probably more so) and the more opportunities there are to celebrate existence the better! For, as far as I can see, we are all expressions of Consciousness and are instruments through which That can experience and enjoy its own manifestation. Which means that enjoying life and enabling others to do so are the main purpose of living.

This enjoyment is greatly enhanced by discovering that one is not a separate object but at the deepest level one is the 'constant conscious subjective presence' – pure Awareness – Consciousness at rest. For then one ceases to see the world through the filter of self-interest, opinions, judgements, self-aggrandizement (or loathing) etc. Once this filter is removed existence appears much more vivid, radiant and joyful than before. One also then sees others as of being the same essence as oneself and wishes them to enjoy life to the full.

This discovery, that one is essentially Pure Awareness, is easily made … see the appendix, but must then be cultivated by continual reawakenings when one 'nods off' and re-identifies oneself as a separate object. As this discovery is so readily available it does not require any particular auspicious day, or circumstance. In fact every moment is equally favourable and once this discovery has taken place then one has the opportunity to go beyond one's karma:

Awareness itself is totally unaffected by anything occurring in it and thus when complete identification with awareness takes place karma is powerless! That is to say that although these old thought patterns continue to come up one will no longer be compelled, or constrained, by them. They will just appear as 'clouds' scudding across the 'sky' of awareness leaving it totally untroubled, for in this case one does not identify with them or take them as indicators of who, or what, one is. In the same way experiences which could be attributed to one's karma, good or bad, lose their power to affect one's underlying equanimity.[23]

Maybe this Awakening is also what is meant by entering the fifth dimension!?!

With regard to miracles, once the filter of the small self is removed then the world is seen to be miraculous moment by moment. Also, when examined, the myriad expressions (and evolutions) of Consciousness are seen to be miracles. So in this paradigm every moment is auspicious and every 'thing' is miraculous, meaning that one need not wait for an auspicious day to begin the journey of self-discovery and one need not hang on to anything as being of more significance than anything else. For everything is significant and full of meaning being varying expressions of the one Absolute Consciousness.

---

[23] C. Drake, *Awakening and Beyond*, 2012, Tomewin, p.91.

To tie this in with my other writings which state that nothing has essential meaning, by this I meant that everything is impermanent and arises in, abides in and finally subsides back into Awareness – Consciousness at rest. Thus essentially no thing exists as a separate entity and therefore cannot have essential meaning. Also all things are of the same essence, and thus have equal (ephemeral) meaning …

About this Sri Ramakrishna said:

> I used to worship the deity in the Kali (Consciousness in motion – the manifestation) temple. It was suddenly revealed to me that everything is Pure Spirit (Consciousness). The utensils of worship, the altar, the door frame – all Pure Spirit. Men, animal and other living things – all Pure Spirit. Then like a madman I began to shower flowers in all directions. Whatever I saw I worshipped. One day while worshipping Siva (Pure Awareness – Consciousness at rest) I was about to offer a bel-leaf on the head of the image when it was revealed to me that this Virat, this Universe, itself is Siva. Another day when I had been plucking flowers it was revealed to me that the flowering plants were so many bouquets adoring the Universal Form of God.[24]

---

[24] The gospel of Sri Ramakrishna p.396

So no special day, bridge, or miracle is needed to Awaken to the fact that at the deepest level one is Pure Awareness – Consciousness at rest – housed in a body/mind which is an expression of cosmic energy – Consciousness in motion. After this Awakening has occurred then there is the possibility to experience that every moment is auspicious and every thing is a miracle, and also that every moment is available to celebrate existence!

To conclude here is a poem celebrating existence in which the play of Consciousness is denoted by the term 'Beloved' and has been given human qualities so that the (my) human mind may relate to and love This.

Dawnsong

The glorious sunrise,
And new day,
The Beloved arising.

The dawn chorus,
Enriching the silence,
A hymn to The Beloved.

The inspiring words,
That I am reading,
The Beloved whispering.

The Miraculous and The Auspicious

The gentle breeze,
Cooling my face,
The caresses of The Beloved.

The exotic fragrance
Of frangipani,
The Beloved's perfume.

The taste of honey,
In morning coffee,
The sweetness of The Beloved.

The ruddy sphere,
Rising from the ocean
The Beloved radiating.

The azure blue,
Of the heavens,
The colour of Her eyes.

The lacy clouds,
Scudding across the sky,
The Beloved exhaling.

The verdant green,
Of hills and forest,
The garden of The Beloved.

The Miraculous and The Auspicious

The sun-shower,
That astonishes,
The Beloved splashing.

The diaphanous rainbow,
A luminous necklace,
Bejeweling The Beloved.

The golden glow,
All around,
The Beloved beaming.

The enveloping warmth,
Of early sunshine,
The embrace of the Beloved.

This doggerel,
An attempt at,
A tribute to The Beloved.

All that is,
Including the writer,
The Beloved.

Chapter 15

The Apparent Elasticity of Time

An attempt to explain the apparent elasticity of time that is encountered after Awakening.

I recently received the following question from one of my readers:

> 'Am I on the right track in thinking that when these thoughts, opinions and like relent the mind is then free to focus on the task at hand......as any good computer should when uncluttered from virus and malware?'

As with most good questions it contains its own answer. For life is managed much more efficiently when approached with a still mind, as then the mind is used in its true capacity, as a problem solving (and working) device, it is much more efficient when it can concentrate solely on the task in hand. This is directly related to self-identity, for identifying oneself as a separate object (in a universe of such) leads to existential angst, self-absorption, considering one's self-interest, opinions, judgements, worrying about one's self-image etc ... These all occupy the mind disturbing its stillness and run as a multitude of background programs when the mind is called onto act in its working capacity. Naturally this makes the mind inefficient, just as a computer can solve a complex problem much more quickly when running a single program compared to when it is running many programs simultaneously.

The simple solution to this is to discover the constant, conscious, subjective presence (pure awareness) that one actually is ... see the appendix, and cultivate identification with This. For this then terminates the 'background programs' as they are seen to relate to a non-existent entity! When this occurs time seems to acquire a seemingly miraculous quality, that of elasticity, as one is able to achieve a great deal with minimal effort and no waste of time.

As an example of this I have a tendency to be lazy, spending on average at least two hours of my 'waking' day lying down: meditating, contemplating, relaxing, 'wobbling' (on a Zen-Chi massager) and sometimes just dozing! I also spend as much time as I can each day hanging out on the verandah, enjoying the glorious view, eating, drinking, reading and entertaining guests. This would amount to at least another two hours a day and much more when friends are present. In fact I am sure many casual acquaintances think that this is all I do as this is all they ever experience of my activities! Add to this 2-3 hours of TV each evening and sometimes much more in the day when international cricket, or champions league soccer is showing, plus the large amount of time Janet and I spend travelling and holidaying in our campervan each year it's a wonder that I ever get anything done!

Yet to balance this in the last ten years there has been the completion of a full-time four year honours degree in comparative religion and philosophy, the (researching, writing, editing and) publication of seven books, writing new articles and poems and answering questions by my readers, running a successful part-time pottery making restaurant ware, volunteering at the local environment centre as their IT and Volunteer

The Apparent Elasticity of Time

Co-ordinator, maintaining an old large farmhouse and macadamia plantation of over 300 trees, maintaining three old vehicles and various pieces of farm machinery plus the usual tasks of living such as shopping, cooking, managing household finances, playing golf with my son, carrying out a regular morning yoga routine, and helping with the housework etc…

In fact it truly does appear to me that time is elastic in that one can achieve whatever one desires whilst still allowing plenty of time for relaxation and spiritual 'practices' … A lot of this is down to efficient time-management but there are other elements. Another of these that is enhanced by the quiet mind is intuition and flowing on from this lateral-thinking. For intuitions can often be very subtle and easily obscured by the background programs that are running, and when the mind is uncluttered this makes lateral thinking much easier. I recently read on Facebook that 'The conscious mind can process 16 bits per second; the unconscious mind can process 11 million bits per second!'. So it can be readily seen that, when the conscious mind is quiet, problems may be more efficiently solved by the unconscious mind (intuition).

This, plus lateral-thinking, greatly enhance our problem solving ability resulting in considerable time savings. All of the above are reliant on the major factor, which is not identifying oneself as a separate object with all of the useless suffering, mind-spinning and time-wasting this causes. Needless to say another benefit of avoiding this is that life becomes much less stressful and exhausting, resulting in one needing less sleep and saving even more time!

Take today as a typical example of how one can cram so much into a short space of time:

5.30 - 5.45 Arising after 6 hours in bed. Morning ablutions.

5.45 – 6.30 Early morning sitting reading spiritual books on the verandah with a strong coffee.

6.30– 7.30 Meditation/contemplation lying in the campervan.

7.30 – 8 Answering e-mails, particularly the question at the beginning, and financial management.

8 -8.20 Morning physical yoga.

8.20 – 8.45 Cooking breakfast for Janet and I.

8.45 – 9.15 Sitting on the verandah eating breakfast and talking.

9.15 – 9.45 Writing this article.

9.45 – 10.45 Moving furniture, working at the pottery and car maintenance.

10.45 – 12.00 Painting the alcove behind our wood stove.

12.00 – 12.30 Watching the first cricket Test Match between Australia and Sri Lanka.

12.30 – 1.10 Wobbling on the Zen Chi massager followed by yoga-nidra.

1.10 – 1.30 Fixing the computer.

1.30 – 2.10 Lunch, on the verandah, whilst doing the daily crossword with Janet.

2.10 – 2.30 Finishing the painting.

2.30 – 3.00 Watching more cricket.

3.00 – 3.30 Finishing this article!

Now I am going back to the pottery and then (Inshallah): a shower, more coffee/reading on the verandah, followed by contemplation in the van, food preparation, dinner (on the verandah), washing up, the evening's TV watching, teeth brushing, wobbling, contemplation and bed ... Another glorious day over!!

One final point is that when the 'background programs' are terminated by the realisation that one is Pure Awareness, and that no separate self exists, then one approaches (and carries out) each task with no attachment or desire for a particular result. This is true 'Karma Yoga' (union through disinterested action) as delineated by Sri Krishna in the Baghavad Gita; but it is the result of, rather than a path to, Awakening. In this one meets life with a quiet mind, ready to respond to any challenge, and each task is performed with relative efficiency, no 'second thought' (caused by relating to an illusory 'me') or needless indecision. Thus one lives in the 'eternal now' which is not bound by (the human conception of) time...

Needless to say this is only the case when one is Awake, as soon as one misidentifies as an apparently separate being one finds oneself back in the time-bound illusion, and I would like to reiterate that I continually flip-flop between wakefulness and sleep, so sometimes time appears to be elastic and at other times it appears fixed.

Chapter 16

The Final Obstacle to Freedom

Discusses the (apparent) 'final obstacle' to Awakening and the importance of one's thought processes in achieving freedom.

The Final Obstacle to Freedom

It is generally thought that freedom, moksha, nirvana (call it what you will) is difficult to achieve and takes a long time. There is the well known story, attributed to Buddha, which says that it can take as long as it would for a bird to wear away Mount Everest by flying back and forth and stroking it with a silk scarf! In the eastern religions, which believe in reincarnation, it is generally perceived to take many lifetimes and one is encouraged to strive in this life to obtain a more auspicious birth to make spiritual progress. Talking to friends it is held by the majority that glimpses of Awakening are quite rare and that one is normally governed by conditioning and the 'small self'.

Whereas, I have discovered that these glimpses are readily available by investigating the nature of one's day to day experience, see appendix, which reveals that at the core of one's being is Pure Awareness and this is the constant conscious subjective presence that we essentially are! When one identifies with this the 'small self' is seen to be an illusion fostered by the ego and identification with the mind. This misidentification readily reasserts itself, due to many years of conditioning, requiring further investigation for another glimpse.

However, this is as easy as pie, and is worth the (minimal) effort, for the freedom that is felt during the reawakening is wonderfully relaxing. In this the burden of day-to-day living is instantly lifted giving a great feeling of en-lightenment … in the literal sense of the word. So what if you shortly revert to the small self, when you pick the load back up again, for this sense of life being a burden can be used as a symptom that misidentification has reoccurred which can be used to stimulate further reinvestigation.

So initially there is a constant flip-flop between being Awake and asleep, but this is certainly better than remaining asleep constantly careworn by unnecessary mental suffering. As time goes on the periods of Awakening will gradually lengthen and the 'ease of being' will grow stronger. This does require vigilance not to sink back into the old stories perpetuated by (and the perpetuation of) the separate self, and cultivation of Awakening by repeated investigation. This, itself, only takes a split second for as soon as the mind starts up with its stories (which causes unnecessary suffering) then notice that there is effortless awareness of these thoughts; and further than that you are this subjective awareness whilst thoughts and sensations are just as flow of ephemeral objects appearing in that.

Some of the main obstacles to this are the thought that this is difficult, or that I am unworthy of this, or that I am normally asleep and unable to do this, or that I am a separate object or that I am bound, or that I am any thing etc… These thoughts can appear to be very powerful and act as barrier to Awakening, whereas in fact they are all rubbish … as Papaji used to say: 'the final obstacle to Awakening is that you think there is an obstacle'.

As it says in the Dhammapada:

> Ch1 v. 1: Our life is shaped by our mind; we become what we think. Suffering follows an evil thought as the wheels of a cart follow the oxen that draw it.

> Ch1 v. 2: Our life is shaped by our mind; we become what we think. Joy follows a pure thought like a shadow that never leaves.[25]

In this case the thought that I am a separate object (or the ego or mind/body) is the 'evil' thought, whilst "I am Pure Awareness' is the 'pure' thought. This is backed up by the first stage of the Bodhisattva Path when one has glimpsed Awakening which is called 'the joyful'. About the mind Ramakrishna said:

> Bondage is of the mind, and freedom is also of the mind. A man is free if he constantly thinks 'I am a free soul. How can I be bound whether I live in the world or in the forest? I am a child of God, who can bind me?' By repeating with grit and determination 'I am not bound I am free', one really becomes so – one really becomes free.[26]

And Swami Vivekananda, his great disciple, added:

---

[25] E.Easwaran, The Dhammapada,1986,Berkeley,p.87
[26] M.Gupta, The Gospel of Ramakrishna,1942,Mylapore,p.138

> We are ever free if you would only believe it, only have faith enough. You are the soul (the Atman – Pure Awareness) free and eternal, ever free, ever blessed. Have faith enough and you will be free in a minute. ... Therefore proclaim your freedom and be what you are – ever free, ever blessed.[27]

Luckily we do not need faith as we can discover that we are Pure Awareness in an instant by investigating the nature of our direct moment-to-moment experience.

---

[27] Sw. Vivekanandan,The Complete Works Vol 6,1989,Delhi, p.93

Chapter 17

Awakening and Ethics

Considers whether ethics are important in the process of Awakening, or whether they are an outcome of this.

'And He who defines his conduct by ethics,

Imprisons his song-bird in a cage'

Kahlil Gibran from the chapter on religion in *The Prophet*.

'Once The Way is lost then virtue (needs to be cultivated),

Virtue lost then compassion, after that morality,

When lost there's etiquette, the husk of all good faith.'

Tao Te Ching verse 38.

'The Way brings forth virtue' (v.51)

'Cultivate The Way and your virtue will be genuine' (v.54)

All religions try to impose a moral code on their followers, some with the aim of preventing them from 'sinning' and others as aids to Awakening. The religions 'of the book' have the ten commandments plus injunctions from the Torah, Jesus and Mohammed. Hinduism has the various rules from the Vedas, plus the Yamas and Niyamas - the ethical precepts set forth in Patanjali's Yoga Sutras as the first and

Awakening and Ethics

second of the eight limbs of yoga, and various other rules stipulated by the many different sects. Whereas, Buddhism suggests the Noble Eightfold Path as the means to attain Nirvana. Now the writer, philosopher and pillar of the Fourth Estate, Alain de Botton, has just published a set of 10 commandments for virtuous atheists, which are designed to make for a more humane society. His list is as follows:

1. Resilience: Keeping going even when things are looking dark.
2. Empathy: The capacity to connect imaginatively with the sufferings and unique experiences of another person.
3. Patience: We should grow calmer and more forgiving by being more realistic about how things actually happen.
4. Sacrifice: We won't ever manage to raise a family, love someone else or save the planet if we don't keep up with the art of sacrifice.
5. Politeness: Politeness is closely linked to tolerance, -the capacity to live alongside people whom one will never agree with, but at the same time, cannot avoid.
6. Humour: Like anger, humour springs from disappointment, but it is disappointment optimally channelled.
7. Self-awareness: To know oneself is to try not to blame others for one's troubles and moods; to have a sense of what's going on inside oneself, and what actually belongs to the world.
8. Forgiveness: It's recognising that living with others is not possible without excusing errors.
9. Hope: Pessimism is not necessarily deep, nor optimism shallow.

10. Confidence: Confidence is not arrogance - rather, it is based on a constant awareness of how short life is and how little we will ultimately lose from risking everything.[28]

Whilst this is a very worthy list is it actually possible to develop these attributes by force of will alone? And if one attempts this how does this affect one's spontaneity and joie de vivre? It seems to me that, while certain rules are obviously necessary to maintain a civilized society, to actually attempt to create the 'virtuous man' without some degree of Awakening taking place is an impossible task.

This is especially true if one defines oneself as a separate object in a universe of such, for then one tends to treat others as objects (for that is what one thinks they are!), the results of which we can see quite clearly in the world around us. Whereas, if one discovers the constant conscious subjective presence, Pure Awareness, that we all are then this problem vanishes. This is easy to do by directly investigating our moment-to-moment experience, see the appendix, after which we see others as of the same essence as ourselves. This directly leads to treating all alike and greatly enhances our ability to manifest the 'virtues':

1. Resilience: Pure Awareness is unaffected by its environment and thus no resilience is required, or you could say resilience comes naturally.
2. Empathy: One can only display true empathy when one sees the other as oneself.

---

[28] http://www.smh.com.au/lifestyle/life/the-10-commandments-for-atheists-20130205-2dw83.html#commandments

3. Patience: When one is identified with Pure Awareness then there is no separate self to become impatient.
4. Sacrifice: Who is sacrificing what? We are all manifestations of the one Consciousness and thus any thing done for 'another' is done for ourselves.
5. Politeness: Politeness is natural as we are not dealing with 'others'. It is true that most will not share our viewpoint, but this leads to compassion for their unnecessary mental suffering caused by misidentifying themselves as separate objects in a universe of such.
6. Humour: Is natural when the universe is seen to be the play of Consciousness, of which we are expressions acting in the play.
7. Self-awareness: To know that one is Pure Awareness is to be aware of The Self.
8. Forgiveness: Most errors are caused by ignorance (misidentification), or lack of awareness, which is natural as this is the state of the majority of humanity. So when one is identified as Pure Awareness these errors elucidate compassion rather than blaming or judging. In this case no forgiveness is necessary.
9. Hope: When identified with Pure Awareness no hope is required, as This never needs anything to be different…
10. Confidence: When one is identified with The Self then Self-confidence is the outcome, not confidence in the imaginary small limited self but confidence in the true Self – Pure Awareness.

Thus these attributes are the outcomes of Awakening, and not the prerequisites for it. This is also true for most of the rules and injunctions that are prescribed by the many different spiritual paths. So I urge you all to Awaken, and to remain Awake by repeated investigation, when no list of prescribed rules or codes will be necessary. Then your 'song-bird' can fly freely for your conduct will not be defined by ethics but by the spontaneity of The Self.

Chapter 18

Staying Awake by The Bodhisattva Vow

This was written in response to a reader who had experienced 'Awakening' but whose mind continued to spin due to its lack of productive engagement with life.

Staying Awake by The Bodhisattva Vow

Here is a recent e-mail encounter with a reader of my books:

From: XXXX
Sent: Sunday, April 07, 2013 8:33 AM
To: Colin Drake
Subject: Oscillation---

Hi Colin,

I haven't written to you in some time, but your writings are still at the foundation of much of my knowledge and practice of non-duality. The problem is, since I've retired, my mind, which was formerly more occupied, has reared its ugly head again in an apparent attempt to regain control of my persona through identification with feelings of failure, depression, anxiety, etc. Since you address this very issue at the beginning of "Beyond the Separate Self", I thought perhaps you might suggest a "modus operandi" for dealing with this situation; even writing this email required me to overcome feelings of torpor, lethargy and shame---perhaps my "self-realization" was neither as authentic of durable as I thought---the Universe seems to have a tendency to bring one down a notch or two when reality doesn't match his perception of spiritual progress. It's quite disappointing, and any thoughts you might have on the subject would be very welcome.

Best Wishes,

XXXX

Staying Awake by The Bodhisattva Vow

From: Colin Drake
Sent: Sunday, April 07, 2013 9:24 AM
To: XXXX
Subject: Re: Oscillation---

Dear XXXX, As I am sure you know I have done nothing but attempt to answer this question. I am sure that you realize that the 'I' and 'me' that is referenced below (in your email) is not the Magnificent Pure Pristine Radiant Awareness that lies at the core of your (all) being, and that it is this constant self-referencing (identified with this 'small self') that reinforces the problem. I have attached the three articles that I feel address your particular problem the best.

   One thing I would also suggest is to find something constructive for the mind to do, for few minds can exist in a vacuum without generating non-existent problems to solve, and as realizing that one is Awareness is extremely simple (see poem) this does not fit the bill! Maybe when one is totally Awake one can live with a silent mind except for when it is called on to solve the problems of day-to-day living, but as modern living presents much fewer of these than formerly this would require an extreme degree of Awakening to live in only this mode. Even on the Bodhisattva path (of Mahayana Buddhism) the stages require the aspirant to constantly engage with the world in an attempt to support the Awakening of all beings. As I am sure you can see this is a never ending problem allowing the mind plenty of scope. In this regard I am extremely lucky ... and you too can be by taking up this challenge helping those you encounter to be aware of a nondual way of looking at the world. I do hope this has been of some help, Love, Colin

From: XXXX
Sent: Sunday, April 07, 2013 10:14 AM
To: Colin Drake
Subject: Re: Oscillation---

Thanks so much, Colin---your response was a great help and an even greater reminder to remain vigilant and avoid complacency!
Love and Peace,
XXXX

This exchange highlights the problem of living with a mind that has insufficient constructive work to keep it content, for as I say in *Beyond The Separate Self*:

> For most of us much of our waking time is spent in obsessive thinking about 'ourselves' and our relationships with other people. This is especially true when we are not working, using our minds in a productive activity; or when we are not relaxing in such a way that engages the mind such as reading a book,

playing a game or watching a screen. For the mind is akin to an onboard-computer which is a wonderful tool for problem-solving, information storing, retrieval and processing, and evaluating the data provided by our senses. However, when it is not fully utilized it tends to search for other problems to solve, and if these are not presently available it tends to speculate about the future, delve into the past, or imagine in the present, creating non-existent problems which it then tries to solve!

Most people tend to identify with their mind, rather than seeing it as a tool, which creates myriad problems. This causes everything to be seen through the filter of the mind: its opinions, judgements, and self-interest. When this happens we cease to see things as they really are which lessens our ability to relate to the world in a natural healthy way. Imagine the problems it would cause if your computer decided that it was 'you' and coloured all the information it retrieved from the internet with its own arbitrary opinions and judgements. In this case you would be unable to rely on any of this information, and if you did then any decisions made using this would be liable to be faulty.[29]

Now it is easy to see that this identification with the mind is greatly exacerbated by having nothing (useful) for the mind to do, unless one is

---

[29] C. Drake, *Beyond The Separate Self,* 2009, Tomewin, p.10.

completely 'Awake' when this misidentification is not present. In this case it is possible to live with a silent mind until it is required to solve a problem, plan something or engage in communication with those around us. As such it is in 'working mode' and relapses back into silence when the task in question is completed. However, this is not the case for most of us who flip-flop between being 'Awake', identified with pure Awareness, and being asleep identified as a separate object in a universe of such. In this latter state the unoccupied mind will naturally 'speculate about the future, delve into the past, or imagine in the present, creating non-existent problems which it then tries to solve'.

So it is very beneficial to have a useful activity for the mind to carry out, to prevent this counter-productive speculation. For this speculation, and wallowing in the past, reinforces the sense of a 'separate I', making the periods of 'Awakening' shorter and more infrequent. Moreover, if one can discover a useful activity which satisfies the mind whilst also tending to facilitate 'Awakening' and staying 'Awake' then this is the ultimate win-win scenario! For it overcomes the problem of the mind being "the devil's playground" and instead turns it into "The Absolute's instrument".

One of the best ways to do this is to help facilitate the 'Awakening' of others, when one has flipped to being 'Awake', which in turn keeps one 'Awake' whilst this activity is occurring … another beautiful win-win!! So I would urge you all to take the Bodhisattva Vow which is to aid all beings to 'Awaken' by any means that you can, which also strengthens one's own 'Awakening'… This activity is endless and contains a seemingly infinite number of 'skilful means' to be discovered and utilized, giving the mind plenty of scope to be of genuine use and attain fulfilment.

To round this out here is my correspondents reply:

Hi Colin,

Thanks for the wonderful reply and subsequent poem---they are right on the mark! Things are much better now as I continue my spiritual work and do useful and recreational activities every day. Truly, "Idleness is the devil's playground." At least, at this time in my development, as you point out, constructive activity is a fine remedy for "monkey mind".

In Love and Peace,

XXXX

Chapter Nineteen

Three Questions For Nondualists

This chapter was stimulated by a nondualist who continued to take things personally, act defensively and engage with the world through the filter of his own knowledge.

Three Questions For Nondualists

I recently had an enlightening (for me, not my correspondent) e-mail exchange that brought up three vital questions for non-dualists who consider themselves to have some degree of Awakening. The correspondence was with the person, a promoter of nondualism, who asked the question 'Why write about the ineffable?' which I answered in an article of the same name. When I sent this to him his response was lukewarm, the thrust of which was 'whatever turns you on, but you're basically wasting your time'. He is not the only one to ask me this question and my reply was not addressed to him personally but to all those who wondered about this. It also helped me to crystallize my reasons for writing on the subject of The Absolute.

When I turned the article into a poem (given at the end of this chapter), which I have a penchant for, I sent it to him in the hope that it would clarify the situation. For the poems are sometimes more powerful as they say the same thing in less words and occasionally add something which the original lacked. His response was to take the poem as a personal attack and respond with an angry e-mail which vigorously defended the charges (of which there were none!), belittled my reasons for writing and questioned my own degree of Awakening. I was astonished that anyone could be so sensitive as to take such obviously general statements personally, although I remembered that it had happened once before, and I responded in the same way as I did previously by e-mailing 'It's not about you!!!'

Three Questions For Nondualists

However, there was also some discomfort at the attack on me which indicated that I was also exhibiting a degree of 'taking it personally'. So this brings up the first question:

'Why should a nondualist who has discovered that no separate person exists take anything personally?'

The side effect of this is to wish to defend oneself, from the so-called attack, a temptation which I found easy to resist but which I did note arising. Which brings up the second question:

'Why should a nondualist who has discovered that one is not self-image, ego or body/mind feel the need to be defensive when felt to be under (verbal) attack?

Returning to my e-mail correspondence he replied by asking why I sent it to him, to which I replied:

> Dear ZZZZ, I sent this out to all who asked me this seminal question (Why write about the ineffable?), and due to its importance will forward it to my e-mail group. As I am sure you know it is one of the age old questions which is at the heart of the split between Mahayana and Hinayana Buddhism, between aspiring Bodhisattvas and Arhats. Its antiquity is also shown in the story of Lao-Tzu

who it is said wished to leave his home kingdom and spend the end of his days in the mountains. The king would only permit this if he were to put his wisdom into words to help others, which Lao-tzu had not done for he felt it was impossible. So he finally agreed to try but hedged his bets by starting with the famous first line of the Tao Te Ching, given in the poem.

My poem and article were not aimed directly at any 'personal individual' for, as you know, no such being actually exists! They are just my way of teasing out my own answer to this important question and having done so I felt it only courteous to send it to those who have put it to me. They are an attempt to delineate the reasons for my seeming compulsion to keep writing and I have received many encouraging responses from this endeavour,
Cheers, Colin

To which his response was:

Dear Colin,
I didn't ask because I don't know the answer.
And I have no doubt whatsoever about my own existence.
And I'm fully aware of the limitations of left-brain linguistic analysis and so can't take it too seriously.

You explained in your first email why you write. I didn't need more.

Have a nice day - writing if you like....

ZZZZ

Which leaves me asking why did he ask the question if he (thought he) already knew the answer? In fact such an action is disingenuous, to say the least, for such a questioner will not really hear anything that is being said as he will filter it through his own 'knowing'. Which brings me to the third question:

> *'Why should a nondualist promote their own knowing when the direct experience of existence is clouded if encountered through the mind's filter of previous knowledge?'*

At this point I can hear you saying I know someone who does that (the author!) so this is a classic case of the 'pot calling the kettle black!' Which is exactly the point - that I need to ask these three questions of myself. The answer to this last question brings us back full circle to 'why write about the ineffable?' which I hope the poem answers. Moreover, I always encourage my readers not to take anyone's word on Awakening, or The Absolute, but to investigate for themselves.

Pointers are useful but are only that, discoveries need to be made first hand to be transformative.

So these are the three questions that I feel are vital for nondualists who claim some degree of Awakening to investigate and find the answers within themselves:

Why take anything personally?
Why react defensively when your opinions, or knowing, are challenged?
Why promote your own knowing, without entering into discussions with an open mind?

I have discovered my own answers but I do not wish to prejudice your exploration with these.

In case any of you are thinking that this article might upset ZZZZ you need not worry for he is not on my e-mail list and has since forbidden me to send him any of my 'public writings'!

The value of this exchange was that it brought up these questions, for me, in relation to my own 'Awakening'. So this gives yet another answer to the question 'Why do I write about the ineffable?', which is to aid my investigation by bringing up more topics to be explored, thus allowing me to 'dive deeper'.

Three Questions For Nondualists

Why Write About The Ineffable?

A sophist recently enquired
Why do you write, wasting your time?
For The Absolute, it has transpired,
Is ineffable, not to be captured in rhyme.

'The Tao that can be spoken is not the Tao'
Of the *Tao Te Ching* the first,
Not to be confined by words so how
Can it be elucidated by essay or verse?

But when of Awakening one has discovered the ease,
And that this readily dispels angst and fear,
This must be proclaimed, even it does displease
The perfectionist to whom silence is so dear.

For if of the divine nothing was written or spoken,
And all Awakened beings had remained 'mum',
Of scriptures, or spiritual paths … not even a token,
Would have appeared, or into being come.

A reader recently appreciated my e-mail musing,
On the verge of suicide she was reminded,
Of Pure Awareness, this her despair defusing,

Three Questions For Nondualists

Realizing that we are not by body/mind defined.

The Dalai Lama said that inner tranquillity,
Comes from developing love and compassion,
So such pointings can restore another's serenity,
For Awakening brings these qualities 'into fashion'.

Writing on The Absolute helps one to stay Awake,
Carefree, full of joy, vigour and vim,
By such deeper discoveries one may make,
So that one's Awakening does not grow dim.

Footnotes:

The word 'sophist' was used as it is an ancient Greek word for the group of philosophers with whom it is said that Socrates conversed and debated. The word derives from 'sophos' which means wise, so the word literally means 'wise person' and was employed to give some sense of the antiquity of the question.

The 'perfectionist' will naturally prefer silence as anything said about The Absolute is by definition, imperfect.

Chapter Twenty

Duality and Nonduality

Written to address the apparent paradox of, or opposition between, duality and nonduality ... especially in spiritual experiences.

Duality and Nonduality

I recently had the following e-mail exchange with a good friend which brought up the important question of the experience of duality within the Absolute Reality of which we are all manifestations.

> Hello Colin
>
> As always thank you for sharing your beautiful insights. Have you read the book by a neurosurgeon named Eben Alexander, called 'Proof of Heaven'? It's an easy read about his near death experience. It's quite amazing. He was the typical academic, bow tie wearing non-believer prior to his NDE. Then out of the blue, when he was around 54, he was struck down with E. Coli meningitis and lapsed into a coma for 7 days. His neocortex was totally non-functional and only the very basic parts of his hind brain (reptilian portion) was functioning. This is a quote from his book Page 160 ... <u>At the heart of the most infinite oneness, there was still that **duality**.</u>
>
> He said, he felt a 'oneness' of love with everything, yet he describes God as being an overseeing Higher Power of this loving oneness.
>
> Lots of love XO

On 08/05/2013, at 3:28 PM, "Colin Drake" wrote:

> Dear XXXX, Thanks for that. There is undoubtedly [apparent] duality until the final stillness of nonduality, consciousness at rest. Whilst 'he' was still feeling the

> 'oneness' then there was separation and thus duality. In the final analysis there is no separate being, no 'he' and God, just consciousness and this, by definition, is 'beyond experience' Love, Colin

At this stage I realize I should have written 'apparent duality' and I should also have added that he experienced duality at the heart of the oneness because he was still (and probably always had been) identified as a separate being. This is evidenced by his background before his near death experience. However, this does not invalidate his experience of duality within the oneness for this can be a vital stage prior to the final realization of nonduality.

This is shown by the experiences of Sri Ramakrishna who:

> verified, for him by his own experiences, many diverse Hindu paths, Islam and Christianity. He found that they all lead to at least one of the three aspects of God: the personal in form, the personal without form, the formless with attributes and the formless without attributes. Indeed many of them led to all three, commencing with a vision of God in form, graduating to communion with the formless God with attributes and culminating in complete union with the formless Absolute.[30]

Typical of this experience was the following:

---

[30] C. Drake, *Humanity – Our Place In The Universe,* 2009, Tomewin, p.107-108

On the evening of the third day, whilst in this mood, he saw a man of fair complexion, luminous appearance, with long brilliant eyes and a flat-tipped nose, approaching him. Ramakrishna, charmed by his divine expression, wondered who this could be and as he grew nearer he heard from his own heart the words: 'Jesus The Christ! The great yogi, the loving Son of God, one with the Father, who gave his heart's blood and put up with endless torture, in order to deliver man from sorrow and misery'. The figure then embraced him and merged into him. Ramakrishna then experienced *bhava-samadhi*, a state of ecstasy in which a trace of ego remains, enabling one to enjoy the presence of God. He then lost outer consciousness entering *savikalpa samadhi*, in which one is united with the Absolute with attributes. [31]

So this is an example of experiencing God with form, followed by the formless, but with attributes, in which the feeling of duality still exists so that one may enjoy God's presence. On many other occasions this was then followed by his entering *nirvikalpa samadhi* –'the supreme transcendental state of consciousness in which the spiritual aspirant becomes completely absorbed in Brahman so that all duality is obliterated'.[32]

---

[31] Sw. Saradananda, *Sri Ramakrishna The Great Master,* 1978, Mylapore, p.339
[32] Br. Usha, *A Ramakrishna Vedanta Wordbook*, 1971, Hollywood, p.52

Duality and Nonduality

Therefore we could say that the state that Eben Alexander experienced was that of *savikalpa samadhi* in which there is still the feeling of duality rather than this final stage where all experience and duality ceases. For in this state there is no separate being and thus no one who can experience ...

Beyond this stage of total absorption in nonduality there is another called *sahaj samadhi* in which one lives spontaneously identified as an expression, and instrument, of Brahman. This may sound like it's a long way off but it is actually always present and may be readily accessed by becoming aware of, and identifying with, Awareness. This being the screen on which all of our sensations/thoughts and mental images appear and are 'seen' by the mind, when the mind becomes 'aware' of them.

This is easy to directly experience by closing one's eyes and seeing whether you can simultaneously be 'aware of' (notice) all of the thoughts/mental images and sensations that are occurring. This is found to be impossible and yet these are all there in Awareness, which becomes apparent when one focuses one's mind on , or turns one's mind to, any of them.... and there they are!

Rumi described this as: *the clear conscious core of your being, the same in ecstasy as in self-hating fatigue.* That is to say the Awareness in which the ecstasy or the self-hating fatigue appears. Now generally you would just be aware of, and affected by, the phenomenal state. If, however, you become aware of the Awareness in which this state is occurring and can fully identify with, and as, this Awareness then the state loses its power to affect your equanimity. For Awareness is always utterly still and silent, totally unaffected by whatever appears in it, in the same way that the sky is unaffected by the clouds that scud across it.

It is this identification with Awareness that can be achieved by 'investigation of the Way' and the easiest way to do this is to directly investigate the nature of one's moment-to-moment experience, see the appendix. When this is successfully accomplished and you can see that at the deepest level, <u>you are Awareness itself</u> then this is an Awakening. If this cultivated by remaining 'aware of Awareness' (and identified as Awareness) then this leads to full Awakening.

This Awareness is not personal but is common to all and is the 'constant conscious subjective presence' that is consciousness at rest; from which all matter/energy which is consciousness in motion (or motion in consciousness) arises, in which it abides and subsides. In this there is no duality as there is only the one essence, consciousness, appearing in two modes at rest and in motion. To back up my assertion that all things arise in, exist in, are seen by, and finally subside back into pure Awareness (consciousness at rest) this can be shown to be the case at the purely experiential level, see the appendix, in particular point 7.

Duality and Nonduality

If you can sink deeply into this pure awareness (in which the following arise, reside and subside) it's easy to see that thoughts, sensations, mental images, feelings of separation etc. are just a flow of ephemeral objects coming and going, ebbing and flowing, tooing and froing, hiding and showing in that constant conscious subjective presence (pure awareness) that we all are.

To give another angle to the duality/nonduality paradox I include the following poem which highlights the purpose of our (apparent) separation, its final dissolution and the problem with identifying as a separate being ... not necessarily in that order:

The Myth of Ego (Separation)

The myth of ego is pervasive,
Seeming inescapable, useful or an 'advanced state',
These ideas are very persuasive,
Held by the majority of those to whom I relate.

Alas it's often with 'character' confused,
Or with personality equated,
Thus with apparent reality it's imbued,
And its value is grossly inflated.

Actually it's an illusory concept,
The major cause of misidentification,
Positing that one is a separate object,
Rather than an ephemeral manifestation.

Duality and Nonduality

Of consciousness we are a fleeting emanation,
Possessing a unique body and mind,
Through which That can experience Its creation,
Enjoying the thoughts and sensations we 'find'.

To live in a useful and harmonious way,
We need character and personality,
Attributes of each expression, day to day,
Until finally merging back into the Totality.

So apparent separation and its properties,
Are impermanent, not applying to The Absolute,
Needed to encounter the world's diversities,
Until back into Aware Nothingness we transmute.

Thus character and personality are needed,
But not ego nurturing separation,
By which universality appears impeded,
In fact it's just the mind's fabrication.

Chapter Twenty One

The Seer, Knower and Enjoyer

Addresses three 'properties' of The Absolute, give in the Upanishads, those of Seeing, Knowing and Enjoying. It attempts to show that each of these may be used as a path to Self-realization.

The Seer, Knower and Enjoyer

One of the epithets for Brahman (the Absolute Reality, Pure Awareness) given in the Upanishads is 'The Seer, Knower and Enjoyer'. This is because everything experienced by all beings (manifestations of cosmic energy – consciousness in motion) appears in this Awareness (consciousness at rest) exists in This, is seen by This and subsides back into This. For all motion arises from stillness, exists in (and is known relative to) stillness and finally subsides back into stillness. Thus everything seen, known and enjoyed (by all) is seen by Awareness, which is by definition aware of these, thus making this Pure Awareness the ultimate Seer, Knower and Enjoyer.

> This is pointed to by Advaita Vedanta which regards man as a physical organism through which Brahman (awareness, consciousness) senses and experiences the world. The Kena Upanishad states that it is the Self (Brahman, awareness) which is the agent and witness, through which the mind thinks and the senses experience sensations. However this Self is undetectable by the mind and senses, being the substratum in which they appear, exist and disappear. (Kena Upanishad 1v.1-9) Moreover, due to its undetectable nature, it is very easy for man to overlook his true nature and identify with the mind and body. The Katha Upanishad likens man to a chariot, of which the atman (the Self, awareness, Brahman within each individual) is the master, the body is the chariot, the mind is the charioteer, the

sense organs are the horses and the roads they travel on are the objects of sensation. The atman is the enjoyer and experiencer of the ride, which is made possible by the charioteer, chariot and horses. (Katha Upanishad 3v.3-4) So Brahman needs the mind and senses, to enjoy and experience the physical world. However when the mind is unaware of the master's presence, through lack of discrimination, it is unable to control the senses which run amok like wild horses (Ibid 3v.5). Brahman, pure consciousness, is hidden in every heart, being the eternal witness watching everything one does. He is said to be 'the operator' whilst we are his 'innumerable instruments'. (Svetasvetara Upanishad 6v.10-12) [33]

As Brahman is the 'Seer, Knower and Enjoyer' of which we are ephemeral manifestations it stands to reason that seeing, knowing and enjoying should represents ways in which we can realize our essential nature as Pure Awareness – Brahman.

Seeing (with the mind – 'spiritual vision') means realizing, or recognizing, and this is key to Raja Yoga known as 'The Kingly Way' which emphasises meditation to still the mind so that one may see one's real nature (Ch1v3, Ch2v28 & v44). This leads to seeing the 'Inner Light' (Ch2v52) and 'vision of Samadhi' (Ch3v9) which leads to enlightenment - seeing the light – (Ch3v33-34). From this comes

---

[33] C. Drake, *A Light Unto Yourself,* 2010, Tomewin, p.50-51

discrimination, seeing the difference between the real and the unreal, which leads directly to liberation (Ch4v25-34).[34]

Knowing is the way of Jana Yoga, the path of obtaining knowledge of The Absolute by self-inquiry and direct investigation of Reality. The easiest way to achieve this is by investigating one's own moment-to-moment experience, see the appendix, which is all we have (to investigate) in the final analysis ... as our whole life is just a series of experiences and everything we encounter is just an experience (to us). This lead to discovering that there is only Pure Awareness (consciousness at rest) in which all sensations, thoughts, mental images (our experience of 'things') arise, abide, are spied and subside. This ephemeral flow of objects are just expressions of cosmic energy (consciousness in motion) which eventually must return back to (consciousness at) rest – Pure Awareness. Thus there is only Brahman of which all is a fleeting manifestation.

Enjoying is what Tantra is all about, not rejecting anything in manifestation but using everything that is encountered as a potential vehicle to achieve liberation. For these are all forms of cosmic energy, Sakti (*The Lila*), consciousness in motion, the consort of Siva (Pure Awareness - *The Nitya*), consciousness at rest. As can be seen these are

---

[34] These chapter and verse numbers are all from *The Yoga Aphorisms of Patanjali* given in:
Sw Prabhavananda & C. Isherwood, *How to Know God*, Vedanta Soc of S. California, 1953

both aspects of the one Absolute Reality (Brahman) but whereas in the two previous paths the emphasis is on *The Nitya*, in Tantra it is on *The Lila* – the play of God. For the universe is regarded as the play of Sakti and Siva and these **are** Brahman thus knowledge of one's absolute unity with This may be obtained from worshipping (or investigating) either of these aspects.

If viewed in a certain way, everything that we perceive, that is, every thought and sensation can directly reveal the nature of Reality. For there are two underlying principles that lie at the heart of each perception, without which it would be impossible for any perception to occur. These are awareness and nothingness, for we would not know that a perception has occurred without being aware of it, and perception of any 'thing' only occurs relative to the nothingness in which it occurs.

Now The Absolute Reality consists of consciousness in two modes – at rest as Pure Awareness and in motion as cosmic energy, the manifest universe. The first of these is unchanging and is the Aware Nothingness in which all things arise and subside. Thus the two Absolute properties of Reality are awareness and nothingness which can be revealed by considering the, aforementioned, two underlying principles that lie at the heart of each perception. So everything can directly reveal the Absolute Reality of which it is an ephemeral manifestation.

Chapter Twenty Two

The Question of 'Sin

This chapter considers the concept of 'sin' and offers a new definition of this which would apply equally well to all religions, tribes and cultures.

The Question of 'Sin'

Having been born into a devout Christian (Methodist) household I heard the word 'sin' often, especially from the pulpit. In fact it often seemed that most of one's thoughts and actions fell into this category. So much so that by the time I was thirteen, and at a Methodist boarding school, I had decided that it was all humbug ... especially when one considered the way that many so called 'Christians' acted, and have acted throughout history.

Since leaving school, and for the last forty years, I have been immersed in Eastern religions, which use the word *avidya* (ignorance) rather than sin. I have always felt this to be a more accurate term with less judgemental overtones. However, I am presently reading 'Return To The Centre' by Bede Griffiths a Benedictine monk who has lived in India in a Christian ashram (which he started) for many years. It is a beautiful book but contains the word 'sin' many times which has made me reappraise my opinion of the concept, which I would like to define as 'Self Image Nourishing' or 'Separate Identity Nurturing'.

This seems to me to be the 'original sin' caused by (eating the apple of) discursive knowledge, that of separation, objectification, analysis and judging" which is borne out by the biblical account in Genesis chapter three. This is covered in an earlier article 'Ego is Misidentification' and here are a few stanzas from the poem on this:

The Question of 'Sin'

> In the biblical tale Adam and Eve were unworried,
>
> About being naked, before the apple they ate,
>
> After, when God appeared, to 'dress' they hurried,
>
> When identified as mind/body and so separate.

> This caused Jehovah to cast them out,
>
> Of the Garden and so their suffering began,
>
> So this myth is an allegory about,
>
> Self image and the trouble it can cause to 'man'.

This nurturing of separation, or self-image, is the cause of much unnecessary suffering both to oneself and others. For this causes one to identify oneself as a separate object (in a universe of such) thus tending to treat others as such, the results of which can be clearly seen in the modern world. It is also the root of 'self grasping' which Buddhism gives as the cause of Dukkha (suffering) and which is to be overcome to achieve nirvana. This subject was expanded in 'Separation is Suffering' in *A Light Unto Yourself*:

> Separation, that is viewing oneself as a separate being (object) in a universe of separate beings (objects) leads inexorably to

suffering. Not mental and physical pain for these are part of the human condition, and thus unavoidable, but unnecessary mental suffering. Which is thinking and worrying about one's self-image, health, wealth, status, achievements, lack of achievements, past, future and ultimate survival. These are all caused by identifying oneself as an individual object in a universe of multiple objects, and also by comparing oneself with like objects (other people). How we identify ourselves is at the heart of how we view the world and our place in it. If we fail to correctly identify 'what we are' (in essence) then this leads to an unfulfilled life, with its consequent frustrations and mental suffering.

When we identify ourselves as 'separate beings' we tend to expand our concept of self-identity to include an imaginary self-image consisting of our physical appearance, mental ability, status, occupation, position in society, family situation, achievements, lack of achievements, ambitions, hopes, fears, memories and projections into the future. This naturally leads to feelings of separation and isolation; separation from our fellow man and the world we live in. Which further engenders feelings of insecurity, and fear. We tend to combat these by trying to improve this imaginary self-image, by attempting to 'better ourselves', achieve more - knowledge, possessions, power, fame, etc. - polish this self-image and generally build ourselves up. This tends to make us live in the future and stops us living fully in the present moment. The other side of this coin is to live in regret as to what might have been, self-loathing, melancholy or nostalgia and yearning for the past. This, once again, stops us seeing 'what is' here and now, either by making us live in the past or by the mind spinning on our failures and lack of self-worth.[35]

Now 'sin' is defined in The Concise Oxford English Dictionary as 'an immoral act considered to be a transgression against divine law' or 'an act regarded as a serious offence'. However, 'immoral acts' or 'serious offences' are not objective realities, but are subjective concepts. They vary greatly in different religious, cultural, racial, national and tribal settings. There are many behaviours that are (or were) considered to be good (or OK) in one of these, whilst considered to be evil in others. Examples are adultery, cannibalism, pedophilia, torture, homosexuality, meat-eating, bigamy, etc., the list is almost endless. It is also apparent that 'divine law' is defined differently by many religions and tribes.

Bearing this in mind it can be seen that 'sin' cannot be an objective reality unless it is given a definition that can apply to all religions, cultures and tribes. Now, as previously discussed, identifying oneself as a separate object, that is with one's self-image, causes unnecessary suffering to oneself and others and it seems to me that would satisfy the definition we are searching for. For all ideologies would agree that causing unnecessary suffering (to oneself or others) is to be avoided, even if they would vary in their definitions of what 'unnecessary suffering' entails. So I would posit that 'Self Image Nourishing' or

---

[35] C.Drake, *A Light Unto Yourself*, 2011, Tomewin, p.45-46

The Question of 'Sin'

'Separate Identity Nurturing' is a definition of 'sin' which would apply universally as the suffering that this causes is not restricted to any religion, tribe or culture, but is common to all.

Chapter Twenty Three

Two Modern Views of The Divine

Considers two modern views of the Absolute Reality by the mystic Georges Bataille and the feminist philosopher Luce Irigaray. It discusses the resonances between their views and those elucidated in previous chapters. It also compares their insights with those of the thirteenth century Christian mystic Marguerite Porete (the author of *The Mirror of Simple Souls*) and her peer the wonderful Sufi poet Jelaluddin Rumi.

Two Modern Views of The Divine

This chapter will consider the ways in which two spiritual luminaries of the twentieth century, the quasi-Christian mystic Georges Bataille and the feminist philosopher Luce Irigaray, conceive of the divine. These views will be compared and contrasted with those of the medieval Christian mystic Marguerite Porete and the thirteenth century Sufi (Islamic) mystic Jalalu'd-Din Rumi. This comparison will highlight any consistencies, similarities or dissimilarities in these views. It will also show how they each rely on two different elements of the Absolute Reality (Consciousness) that we have discovered in the previous chapters.

Firstly, we must define our terms starting with the word 'conceive' which is given in the Compact Oxford English Dictionary as 'devise in the mind, imagine'[36], and 'the divine' which is defined as 'providence or God'[37]. Further 'providence' is given as 'the protective care of God or nature as a spiritual power'[38] whilst God has two meanings: 'the creator and supreme ruler of the universe' and 'a superhuman being or spirit worshipped as having power over nature and human fortunes.'[39] So the phrase 'conceive of the divine' amounts to the way that one thinks about, or mentally pictures, God as the 'supreme ruler and creator' and/or, as the 'spiritual power over (and/or in) nature' and also

---

[36] *Compact Oxford English Dictionary*, Oxford, 2003, p. 220.
[37] *Ibid*, p. 318.
[38] *Ibid*, p. 911.
[39] *Ibid*, p. 474.

the way that one thinks about 'the protective care' which this God or spiritual power exerts over us.

Georges Bataille's mysticism was driven by the 'desire to be everything, to identify with the entirety of the universe'[40], that is the desire to become one with the spiritual power that permeates the universe. However, if one is identified as a separate individual this is not possible as Bataille realised when he wrote 'just as inevitable as the desire to be everything is the knowledge that we will die, that our individual existence is not commensurate to the universe with which we seek identification'[41]. So the only way to truly realise this oneness with the universe is to lose the identification with the 'separate self' and identify with the 'universal self (or power)'. However, this 'loss of (separate) self' is not easy to achieve, especially in the Christian tradition where one is thought to be an individual soul. This requires the 'death of God' as a separate 'creator and supreme ruler'; for Bataille 'the loss of God is the loss of self, the definitive shattering of the anthropic image' resulting in 'an ecstasy that is the experienced loss of being'[42].

His inability to maintain this 'loss of self' resulted in despair when re-identification as an 'individual self' occurred. This led to Bataille

---

[40] Georges Bataille, 'Inner Experience', in Phwg313 *Unit Resources*, Armidale, 2005, p.164.
[41] *Ibid*, p. 164.
[42] Adrian Gargett, *Georges Bataille*, www.richmondreview.co.uk/features/gargett01.html

negating the Christian (idea of) 'God of despair, give me ... .your heart ....which no longer tolerates that you exist.'[43] However, this did not mean that he negated the divine completely as he experienced ecstasy many times when he lost identification with, and let go of, his 'individual self':

> At the crossing of the rue du Four I became in this 'Nothingness' unknown – suddenly....I negated these gray walls which enclose me, I rushed into a sort of rapture. I laughed divinely....I laughed as perhaps one had never laughed; the extreme depth of each thing opened itself up – laid bare as if I were dead. [44]

In this 'nothingness', becoming 'unknown', the 'gray walls' vanish as these are caused by discursive thinking about the problems of a non-existent self. In this there is great relief and laughter naturally follows as one realises the ridiculousness of taking seriously thoughts about a non-existent object and reading meaning into things that have no meaning. Bataille realised this when he said 'The self in no way matters'[45] and 'realise the universal fulfilment....through the revelation of a universe which exists in a state of play rather than one of

---

[43] *Ibid*
[44] Georges Bataille, 'Inner Experience', in Phwg313 *Unit Resources*, Armidale, 2005, p.178A.
[45] Georges Bataille, 'Inner Experience', in Phwg313 *Unit Resources*, Armidale, 2005, p.186.

obligation'[46]. He also realised that ecstasy and 'letting go' of oneself are synonymous[47], unfortunately his ecstasy turned to despair as soon as he re-identified and started looking for the meaning of his illumination.[48] This oscillation between ecstasy and despair, of which the latter was predominant, led Bataille to look for more extreme and bizarre ways to 'lose himself' through eroticism and violence:

> The orgy is not associated with the dignity of religion... The total personality is involved reeling blindly towards annihilation and this is the decisive moment of religious feeling.[49]

> In essence the domain of eroticism is the domain of violence, of violation. The most violent thing for all for us is death which jerks us out of a tenacious obsession with the lastingness of our discontinuous being.[50]

So anything which 'jerks us out of our tenacious obsession' and reveals that we, as separate individuals, do not exist, such as sexual orgasm (the little death), violence or death, is to be pursued as a way to escape from the anguish (of the dark night of the soul) and return to ecstasy. As

---

[46] Georges Bataille, 'Radio National Encounter', in Phwg313 *Unit Resources*, Armidale, 2005, p.143.
[47] Georges Bataille, 'Inner Experience', in Phwg313 *Unit Resources*, Armidale, 2005, p.187.
[48] Georges Bataille, 'Inner Experience', in Phwg313 *Unit Resources*, Armidale, 2005, p.178A.
[49] Georges Bataille, 'Radio National Encounter', in Phwg313 *Unit Resources*, Armidale, 2005, p.146.
[50] Georges Bataille *'Eroticism'* , http://pers-www.wlv.ac.uk/~fa1871/battext.html

Benjamin Noys said: 'He was more interested with violence as an experience in which one loses oneself'.[51] This loss of oneself leads to ecstasy as the weight of years of discursive thinking about oneself is lifted instantly and one truly 'knows nothing' and sees everything 'as it is', that is not through the filter of the mind and all of its judgements, opinions, preferences and conditioning. So Bataille found that he could not conceive of God as the separate creator, or ruler, of a host of individual beings, for this did not concur with his own religious experiences of ecstasy as a result of 'loss of self'. His desire to 'be everything' is more commensurate with merging with the spiritual power that permeates the universe. He did not tend to put this conception of the divine into words apart from such phrases as 'nothingness' or 'what is'; rather he concentrated on describing the ecstasy attained on 'losing himself', plus the methods he employed to achieve this, and the anguish he encountered on his return to discursive thinking and re-identification.

So Bataille discovered that it was necessary to go beyond the (seeming) separate self and realise that one is (merged with) the universal Self (pure Awareness) to overcome the existential despair that tended to engulf him.

Luce Irigaray also argues for the 'death of God', but whereas Bataille's objections to 'God' are mystical and experiential hers are philosophical

---

[51] Benjamin Noys, 'Radio National Encounter', in Phwg313 *Unit Resources*, Armidale, 2005, p.153.

and psychological. She posits that man (the male) has created God in his own image at the expense of women, enabling man to 'complete his essence', which is impossible for women whilst they define god as male. This is because:

> Man is able to exist because god helps him to define his gender, helps him orient his finiteness by reference to infinity ... in order to become it is essential to have a gender or a (sexuate) essence... to become means fulfilling the wholeness of what we are capable of being.[52]

As 'God' is male this definition of gender, orientation, fulfilment and wholeness in unavailable for women so this God must be redefined in such a way as to be accessible to, and supportive of, both genders. Irigaray argues that the male has appropriated the position of 'subject' for himself, and his God, leaving women always in the position of 'object'. This objectivity prevents the female from identifying with 'God', the eternal subject, thus preventing her from achieving wholeness, so she needs a 'God' which will enable her subjectivity. As Irigaray said: 'If she is to become woman, if she is to accomplish her female subjectivity woman needs a god who is a figure for the perfection of her subjectivity.'[53]

---

[52] Luce Irigaray, 'Sexes and Genealogies', in Phwg313 *Unit Resources*, Armidale, 2005, p.212.
[53] *Ibid*, p. 214.

In search for conception of a feminine divine Irigaray introduces the idea of a 'sensible transcendent(al)' which unites the material and spiritual by requiring 'that transcendence arise from immanence through the mediation of materiality.'[54] For in the transcendence of the male 'God' there is a division of material and spirit in which He is depicted as distant and beyond the material world. However, Irigaray's 'sensible transcendent' entails 'not making transcendence an enemy of nature, but rooting it in the reality of the natural world, corporeal and cosmic.'[55]

Frances Gray says that this means that women should explicitly recognise their own bodies as a condition of the transcendent, and 'what counts for Irigaray is female embodiment as the locus of a feminine Divine.'[56] This Divine should challenge the male 'God' and be born out of women's experiences of embodiment and life such that this Divine is 'the mirror of women'[57]. For Irigaray this would not necessarily supplant the male 'God' but would be that through which women could achieve wholeness, and which would allow men and women to form couples which could love each other as equals:

---

[54] *Luce Irigaray and the Advent of the Divine,* Originally published in *Pacifica* 12.1. (Feb1999)
http://dlibrary.acu.edu.au/staffhome/dacasey/Luce%20Irigaray%20and%20the%20Advent%20of%20the%20Divine.html
[55] Luce Irigaray, *Spiritual Tasks of Our Times,*
www.unites.uqamca/religiologiques/21/21abstracts.html
[56] Frances Gray, 'Essentialism, Social Constructionism and The Divine, in Phwg313 *Unit Notes,* Armidale, 2005, p. lviii.
[57] *Ibid,* p. lxi.

> At the furthest extreme of love it is a question of the divine… A love between the sexes, in which nature and gods are united and fertile, is essential to the discovery of an individual and collective happiness, one which is both empirical and transcendental.[58]

Irigaray never spells out what this feminine divine is, or should be conceived as. This, she says, women need to discover for themselves, and so she concentrates on pointing out the lack of, and need for, such a divine:

> Divinity is what we need to become free, autonomous, sovereign. No human subjectivity, no human society has ever been established without the help of the divine… If women have no God they are unable to either communicate of commune with one another. They need, we need, an infinite if they are to share a little.[59]

With regard to a 'spiritual power over (and in) nature', she is not explicit, however her idea of 'rooting the transcendent in the reality of the natural world' does have echoes of this. At any event this 'spiritual

---

[58] Luce Irigaray, 'Elemental Passions', in Phwg313 *Unit Resources*, Armidale, 2005, p.223.
[59] Luce Irigaray, 'Sexes and Genealogies', in Phwg313 *Unit Resources*, Armidale, 2005, p.213.

power' would have to have two aspects, male and female, with which both men and women can identify.

So she argued that the divine needs to be identified with the subjective presence rather than as an object, and that there is no division between spirit and matter.

Bataille's and Irigaray's unwillingness to elucidate the way that they conceive of the divine makes comparison with other thinkers and mystics particularly difficult. All that can be done is to grasp any hints, or clues, they may have given in their musings on the divine and work with these. In Bataille's 'desire to be everything' and 'loss of self' there are echoes of both Rumi and Porete who both lost themselves in love for the divine and thus became everything. In the words of Rumi - 'in love there's nothing left of me'[60], 'I am filled with you ... there's nothing in this existence but that existence'[61] and:

> When you are with everyone but me you're with no one,
> When you are with no one but me you're with everyone,
> Instead of being so bound up with everyone, be everyone,
> When you become that many, you're nothing, Empty.'[62]

Or, as Marguerite Porete says:

---

[60] Coleman Barks, *The Essential Rumi*, London, 1995, p.101.
[61] *Ibid*, p.131.
[62] *Ibid*, p.28.

> A soul who has become nothing has everything,
> wills nothing and wills everything,
> knows nothing and knows everything.[63]

Even the title of Porete's book 'The Mirror of Simple Souls who are Annihilated...' is echoed by Bataille's 'annihilation... the decisive moment of religious feeling'.

In Bataille's equating of entering into nothingness (or the unknown) with the presence of God there are similarities with Rumi's 'praise to the emptiness that blanks out existence'[64] and Porete's 'nothing' about which she said: 'And through such nothing she is fallen into the certainty of knowing nothing ... and this nothing ... gives her all.'[65]

Bataille's realisation that 'letting go leads to satisfaction, happiness, platitude,'[66] is akin to both Rumi's and Porete's experience that surrendering (in love to the divine) leads to ecstasy. Finally Bataille's attempts to lose himself through eroticism and physical love are also echoed in Porete and Rumi but with a different emphasis. Porete talks of being 'ravished' and disrobing, nakedness, union with the divine lover[67], but these are metaphors for the soul (or self) giving up all self-

---

[63] Michael Sells, *Mystical Languages of Unsaying*, Chicago, 1994, p. 123.
[64] Coleman Barks, *The Essential Rumi*, London, 1995, p.21.
[65] Michael Sells, *Mystical Languages of Unsaying*, Chicago, 1994, p. 129.
[66] Georges Bataille, 'Inner Experience', in Phwg313 *Unit Resources*, Armidale, 2005, p.187.

identity and losing itself in the divine. Rumi's poems are full of explicit sexual images but these are not designed to extol the value of physical intercourse but have a twofold function, one as a metaphor for the ecstasy achieved in the union of the soul with the divine, and the other as a warning against becoming overcome by lust:

> This is the virility of a prophet.
> The Caliph was sexually impotent,
> but his manliness was most powerful.
> The kernel of true manhood is the ability to abandon sensual indulgences.
> The intensity of the Captain's libido is less than a husk
> compared to the Caliphs nobility in ending the cycle of sowing lust ...[68]

When it comes to Irigaray there is even less to work with, especially in comparison to other thinkers, because her approach is so unique, opaque, and open-ended. Her idea of the 'sensible transcendent' which arises 'from immanence through the mediation of materiality' could be read to mean either allowing the wonder of the natural world to lead one to transcendence, or seeing the divine (spiritual power) in materiality itself. Rumi's poems are full of images of the beauty of nature, and in one poem he writes:

---

[67] Michael Sells, *Mystical Languages of Unsaying*, Chicago, 1994, p. 125.
[68] Coleman Barks, *The Essential Rumi*, London, 1995, p.63.

The water is the zikr remembering
There is no reality but God.
There is only one God.[69]

Which could be read to mean that God is (in) everything, even materiality. Porete on the other hand makes no such references and seems to be more intent on totally transcending the material:

> Such a creature says love is better vested by the divine life, of which we have spoken, than she is in her own spirit which was placed in her body in its creation… thus it is better that the Soul be in the sweet country of understanding nothing, where she loves, than she is in her own body to which she gives life. And the freeness of love has such power.'[70]

This indicates that the soul, through love, should transcend the body by entering into union with the beloved (God). Which is in almost direct opposition to the idea of 'female embodiment as the locus of the divine' except in the sense that the soul is (potentially) divine and it was 'placed in her body in its creation'.

In general Porete and Rumi both held a fairly conventional view of God as a monotheistic personal being who was transcendent, but also

---

[69] *Ibid*, p. 114.
[70] Marguerite Porete, 'The Mirror of Simple Souls', in Phwg313 *Unit Resources*, Armidale, 2005, p.104.

immanent, omnipotent, omniscient, omnipresent, creator of everything, with whom one could build a personal relationship and in whom one could finally 'lose oneself' in love. This resulted in 'union with the beloved' after which one is totally free and without care provided one does not re-identify oneself as a separate being (ego). Georges Bataille, on the other hand, also had experiences of 'losing himself' which resulted in ecstasy but could relate to no framework of reference for this loss of self.[71] Thus, when these states ceased he would re-identify as a separate being and question (and doubt) what had just occurred. This led to almost perpetual anguish, the 'dark night of the soul' punctuated by interludes of ecstasy when he managed to find some way of 'losing himself' again. If he had formed a 'framework of reference' so that he could have totally surrendered into 'being nothing', and not constantly re-identified as a separate self, he would have escaped this 'dark night' into the 'clear light' of enlightenment, realisation, freedom ... call it what you will.

Luce Irigaray is in a different category as she is more of a philosopher than a mystic, her writings coming from a philosophical, psychological, viewpoint rather than from an experiential mystical viewpoint. Her conception of the divine, such as it is, is very different from that of the other three and it will be interesting to see how this develops as it is

---

[71] Examples of a 'framework of reference for loss of self' which could have helped are: losing oneself in love with/for the divine, complete submission to God (as in Islam), the concept of *Anatta* (no-self) in Buddhism, and the concept of the unity of *atman* (self) and *Brahman* (Absolute Self) in Vedanta.

enunciated more clearly by herself and her followers. Whilst she does make fairly compelling arguments about the inadequacy of the standard (male) conception of God and the urgent need for the development of the 'feminine divine', she appears not to have realised that the 'subjective identity' she argues for is the 'constant conscious subjective presence' – pure consciousness, from and in which all arises, abides and subsides.

Chapter Twenty Three

The Fundamental Teachings of Buddhism

Explains the fundamental teachings of the Buddha, the four noble truths, and in this shows the resonances between these (teachings) and Awakening by becoming 'aware of Awareness'.

In this essay I am going to discuss the 'four noble truths' (suffering, its cause, it can be overcome, how to do this) described as 'the most fundamental and basic teaching of Buddhism'.[72] Not only is it the most fundamental teaching but also, as Etienne Lamotte noted 'the four noble truths were a teaching that encompassed all of the Buddha's teachings contained in the Theravada canon.'[73] About them the *Dhammapada* says:

> 'Of paths the eightfold is the best; of truths the Noble four are the best ... This is the path; there is no other that leads to the purification of the mind. Follow this path and conquer Mara (death)'.[74]

As we shall see, if each of the truths is investigated deeply, they require knowledge and understanding of the concepts of *anatta* – no self, *anicca* – impermanence, the *kandhas* – the five aggregates, conditioned arising or dependant origination (which itself requires knowledge of *dhamma, kamma* and *reincarnation*), *nibbana* – liberation, mindfulness, *jhanic* meditation, insight meditation and of course *dukkha* – suffering, craving or frustration.

These truths spring directly from the Buddha's quest to find an answer to the problem of suffering from which he had be shielded by his father until he was 29. On discovering that aging, illness and death are

---

[72] Choong M., 'RELS305/405 Buddhism: A History, Lecture Notes', 2004, Armidale, p.11
[73] Anderson C., 'Pain and its Ending', 1999, Richmond, p.3
[74] Easwaran E. 'The Dhammapada, verses 273-274' 1986, Petaluma, p.162

integral in all human life he was deeply shocked and on seeing a sadhu who had renounced the world, in an attempt to transcend this suffering, the Buddha was inspired to do likewise.[75] It is said that, after six years of ascetic practices the Buddha realised the futility of these and, after taking a meal, sat under the Bodhi tree where he vowed to stay until achieving enlightenment. The Buddha, on becoming enlightened realised the 'Four Noble Truths, the heart of his teaching'[76], which he preached in his first sermon. About the liberating power of these truths he said:

> And so long, monks, the vision of knowledge of these four ariyan truths ... was not well purified by me, so long was I not thoroughly Awakened ... But when, monks, the vision of knowledge of these four ariyan truths ... was well purified by me, then was I thoroughly Awakened with the supreme full Awakening.[77]

One member of the audience, Kondanna, is said to have glimpsed *nibbana* by gaining 'experiential insight into the truths taught ... an experiences technically known as stream-entry.'[78]

Thus the four truths are the fundamental core of the Buddha's teachings, realised directly by him, the full understanding and realisation of which can lead directly to *nibbana* i.e. cessation of

---

[75] Gowans C., 'Philosophy of the Buddha', 2003, London, p.18-19
[76] Ibid p.21
[77] Horner I.B., 'Mahavagga 1 in The Book of Discipline Vol 1V', 1971, London, p.15-16
[78] Harvey P., 'Buddhism', 1990, Cambridge, p.23

suffering. They are given in the traditional Vedic form of a doctor's diagnosis and treatment, of an illness. First the malady is described, then its cause, next whether it can be cured and finally the prescribed treatment.[79] So now we will consider them in detail.

The Noble Truth of suffering.

> And this monks is the ariyan truth of dukkha. Birth is *dukkha*, old age is *dukkha*, disease is *dukkha*, dying is *dukkha*, association with what is not dear is *dukkha*, not getting what one wants is *dukkha* – in short the five groups of grasping are *dukkha*.[80]

I have replaced the word 'ill' given in the translation with the original *dukkha* as this has many possible translations such as 'suffering', unsatisfactoriness', stress', frustration', etc. As Friedlander says:

> The Hindi meanings of *dukkha* are quite broad. They include emotional qualities such as sorrow grief, distress, dejection, vexation, regret, annoyance and physical aspects such as pain, misfortune, difficulty and trouble.[81]

So I think we can sum this up by saying that life has many negative facets leading to a variety of painful mental and physical experiences. It is fairly apparent that physical pain is, to a certain extent, unavoidable and it is not this with which the Buddha is concerned, except to the extent that this can be avoided in future incarnations by escaping the

---

[79] Watts A., 'The Way of Zen', 1957, New York, p.66
[80] Horner I.B., 'Mahavagga 1 in The Book of Discipline Vol.1V', 1971, London p.15-16
[81] Friedlander P., 'Buddhism, Past and Present', 2002, La Trobe, p.63

samsaric cycle of birth, death and reincarnation. However physical pain can lead to mental suffering, if incorrectly viewed, and it is the mind with which Buddhist teachings are directly concerned. A clue is given above in 'association with what is not dear is *dukkha* and not getting what one wants is *dukkha*' for these are purely mental states caused by how we view ourselves and the world. Also 'the five groups of grasping' which is translated in Williams as 'the five aggregates of attachment'[82] refer mainly to the mental realm.

These aggregates, known as the *kandhas*, are the 'components of sentient beings (or the world)'[83] and are the aggregates of material form, feeling, perception, activities and consciousness. The last four are mental components and it is these, when combined with attachment or clinging, that cause *dukkha*. It is this clinging that can cause even pleasant states to lead to *dukkha* as everything is impermanent, which the Buddhists call *anicca*, and so bemoaning the loss of, or clinging to, a pleasant state causes *dukkha*. As William Blake says about seeing a beautiful butterfly:

> 'He who binds to himself a joy
> Does the winged life destroy;
> But he who kisses the joy as it flies
> Lives in Eternity's sun rise.'

---

[82] Williams P., 'Buddhist Thought', 2000, Routledge, p.42
[83] Choong M, 'RELS305/405 Buddhism: A History, Lecture Notes', 2004, Armidale, p.12

The Noble Truth of the arising of suffering.

And this, monks, is the ariyan truth of the uprising of *dukkha*; that which craving connected with again-becoming, accompanied by delight and passion, finding delight in this and that, that is to say: craving for sense-pleasures, craving for becoming, craving for de-becoming.[84]

This craving has many aspects one of which is the sense of self-attachment, i.e. attaching to 'phenomena or sense objects as self or as belonging to self'.[85] Which brings us directly to the concept of '*anatta*' which means 'no-self'. According to Buddhism the person is just a composition of the five ever-changing *kandhas* with no essential self, or soul. These continue, life after life (except the material form which is renewed with each birth), until *nibbana* is achieved, when there is no rebirth and the 'illusory' person ceases to be. Thus realisation of the truth of *anatta*, that there is no essential 'me' and thus no 'mine' overcomes this self-attachment, self-grasping or 'I conceit'. Also if one does not realise this and identifies with the 'illusory' person then as the *kandhas* change, i.e. one ages, this causes suffering.

Another part of craving is that caused by sensory experience and attachment to certain experiences. As Williams notes: 'This is seen in the formula for dependent origination (conditioned arising) where it is

---

[84] Horner I.B. 'Mahavagga 1 in The Book of Discipline Vol 1V', 1971, London, p.15-16
[85] Choong M., 'RELS305/405 Buddhism: A History, Lecture Notes', 2004, Armidale, p.12

held that conditioned by the six senses is sensory contact, conditioned by sensory contact is feeling and conditioned by feeling is craving.'[86] The *Dhammapada* points out that this craving cannot be quenched by indulging in sensual passion: 'even celestial pleasures cannot quench the passions.'[87]

Gowans links the 'craving for becoming' with the doctrine of 'eternalism' (i.e. the identification of oneself as an eternal 'individual self') and the 'craving for de-becoming' with 'annihilationism' which is the desire to end the seemingly eternal cycle of suffering by annihilation.[88] In the final analysis the cause of *dukkha* is *avidya*, spiritual ignorance, which is also the first link in the chain of 'conditioned arising'. It is this ignorance of the fundamental principles of *anatta*, no-self, and *anicca*, impermanence (of everything) which causes the whole cycle of 'conditioned arising' and thus *dukkha*. In Harvey we find: 'The series runs: spiritual ignorance > constructing activities > (discriminative) consciousness > mind/body > the six sense-bases > sensory stimulation > feeling > death, sorrow, lamentation, pain, grief and despair. Thus is the origin of this whole mass of *dukkha*.'[89] This provides the clue for overcoming *dukkha* by

---

[86] Williams P., 'Buddhist Thought', 2000, Routledge, p.46
[87] Easwaran E., 'The Dhammapada verse 187' 1986, Petaluma, p133.
[88] Gowans C., 'Philosophy of the Buddha', 2003, London, p.29
[89] Harvey P., 'Buddhism'. 1990, Cambridge, p.55

overcoming this ignorance, which is addressed in the third and fourth truths.

The Noble Truth of cessation of suffering.

'And this, monks, is the ariyan truth of the stopping of ill; the utter and passionless stopping of that very craving, is renunciation, surrender, release, the lack of pleasure in it.'[90]

Thus suffering is overcome when one stops craving by realizing that 'phenomena or sense objects are impermanent ... and empty of self or anything belonging to self'. [91] This cessation of craving leads to escaping from the *samsaric* cycle of conditioned arising and to *nibbana*, as Nagasena pointed out when answering the questions of King Milinda:

> The cessation of craving leads successively to the cessation of grasping, of becoming, of birth, of old age and death, of grief, lamentation, pain, sadness and despair – that is to say the cessation of all this mass of ill. It is this cessation that is Nirvana.[92]

That *nibbana*, or 'Awakening' is achieved by realising the truths of *anicca and anatta*, which leads to the cessation of craving, is also stated in the *Dhammapadda* : 'Him I call a Brahmin who is free from I, me

---

[90] Horner I.B., 'Mahavayya 1 in The Book of Discipline Vol.1V', 1971, London, p15-16.
[91] Choong M., 'RELS305/405 Buddhism: A History, Lecture Notes', 2004, Armidale, p.14
[92] Conze E., Milindapasha in Buddhist Scriptures', 1959, Harmondearth, p.156

and mine, who knows the rise and fall of life. He is Awake: he will not fall asleep again.'[93] One is free from 'I, me and mine' when one realises that there is no essential self, *anatta*, and one knows the 'rise and fall of life' when one realises the truth of impermanence, *anicca*. Many scholars, when discussing this truth, focus on *nibbana* itself as the way of overcoming craving. However *nibbana* is the result of conquering *avidya*, and therefore craving, and this truth says nothing about *nibbana* itself, which is not surprising as the Buddha himself concentrated on the methods for overcoming suffering rather than describing the state that one finally achieves.

The Noble Truth of the way leading to the cessation of suffering.
'And this, monks, is the ariyan truth of the stopping of ill: this Aryan eightfold Way itself, that is to say: right view, right thought, right speech, right action, right livelihood, right effort, right mindfulness, right concentration.'[94]

'Right view' is the knowledge of the 'four noble truths', of impermanence, not-self and of following the 'middle way' between the two extremes of existence and non-existence, or between over indulging in sense-pleasures and self-mortification.[95] Thus 'right view'

---

[93] Easwaran E., 'The Dhammapada, verse 419', 1986, Petaluma, p.199
[94] Horner I.B., 'Mahavayya 1 in The Book of Discipline Vol.1V', 1971, London, p15-16.
[95] Choong M., 'rels' 305/405 Buddhism: A History, Lecture Notes', 2004, 'Armidale, p.14

encompasses all of the other aspects of the 'eightfold path' which lead to this 'knowledge' and to full 'realisation' of the truth of 'not-self' and 'impermanence', resulting in the 'cessation of craving' and *nibbana*.

'Right Thought' is that of detachment, non-malice and non-harming[96] and its importance is stressed in the first two verses of the Dhammapada: 'Our life is shaped by our mind; we become what we think. Suffering follows an evil thought as the wheels of a cart follow the oxen that draw it … Joy follows a pure thought like a shadow that never leaves.'[97]

'Right Speech, Action and Livelihood' relate to telling the truth, not harming others in any way (i.e. by thought, word or deed) and by acting according to one's *dhamma* i.e. following Buddha's teachings.

'Right Effort' is concerned with avoiding and overcoming 'evil, unprofitable states' of mind, whilst generating and cultivating 'profitable states' of mind.[98] 'Unprofitable states' being those that hinder the attainment of *nibbana* whilst 'profitable states' being those that aid it.

---

[96] Ibid
[97] Easwaran E., 'The Dhammapada, verses 1-2', 1986, Petaluma, p78.
[98] Choong M., 'RELS305/405 Buddhism: A History, Lecture Notes', 2004, Armidale, p.15

'Right Mindfulness' is constant Awareness of the body and its sensations, the mind, the thoughts and emotions and all 'physical and mental processes'.[99] This is the basis of *Vipassana*, or 'insight', meditation which leads directly to the realisation of the truths of impermanence and 'not-self'.

Right concentration is to do with '*jhanic*', or 'serenity' meditation and is achieved by 'focussing fully and solely on the meditation object which enables the meditator to ascend the four '*jhanas*' (meditative absorptions) of right concentration.'[100]

In conclusion, we have seen how the discovery of 'The Four Noble Truths' were a direct result of the Buddha's exposure to, and quest to find a solution to, *dukkha*. On their realization, when he achieved *nibbana*, his natural compassion propelled him to teach them to others, so that they might also conquer *dukkha*. We have also seen that to fully comprehend them one needs to understand most of the key concepts that underpin Buddhism. So I think we can safely conclude that 'The Four Noble Truths' do indeed contain the most fundamental and basic teachings of the Buddha.

---

[99] Williams, P. 'Buddhist Thought', 2000, Routledge, p.54
[100] Gowans C., 'Philosophy of the Buddha', 2003, London, p.188

Appendix

Investigation of Experience

This gives the basic format for investigating one's moment to moment experience which leads to the conclusion that, at the deepest level, one **is** Awareness.

Investigation of Experience

Below follows a simple method to investigate the nature of reality starting with one's day-to-day experience. Each step should be considered until one experiences, or 'sees', its validity before moving on to the following step. If you reach a step where you do not find this possible, continue on regardless in the same way, and hopefully the flow of the investigation will make this step clear. By all means examine each step critically but with an open mind, for if you only look for 'holes' that's all you will find!

1. Consider the following statement: 'Life, for each of us, is just a series of moment-to-moment experiences'. These experiences start when we are born and continue until we die, rushing headlong after each other, so that they seem to merge into a whole that we call 'my life'. However, if we stop to look we can readily see that, for each of us, every moment is just an experience.

2. Any moment of experience has only three elements: thoughts (including all mental images), sensations (everything sensed by the body and its sense organs) and Awareness of these thoughts and sensations. Emotions and feelings are a combination of thought and sensation.

3. Thoughts and sensations are ephemeral, that is they come and go, and are objects, i.e. 'things' that are perceived.

4. Awareness is the constant subject, the 'perceiver' of thoughts and sensations and that which is always present. Even during sleep there is Awareness of dreams and of the quality of that sleep; and there is also Awareness of sensations; if a sensation becomes strong enough, such as a sound or uncomfortable sensation, one will wake up.

5. All thoughts and sensations appear in Awareness, exist in Awareness, and subside back into Awareness. Before any particular thought or sensation there is effortless Awareness of 'what is': the sum of all thoughts and sensations occurring at any given instant. During the thought or sensation in question there is effortless Awareness of it within 'what is'. Then when it has gone there is still effortless Awareness of 'what is'.

6. So the body/mind is experienced as a flow of ephemeral objects appearing in this Awareness, the ever present subject. For each of us any external object or thing is experienced as a combination of thought and sensation, i.e. you may see it, touch it, know what it is called, and so on. The point is that for us to be aware of anything, real or imaginary, requires thought about and/or sensation of that thing and it is Awareness of these thoughts and sensations that constitutes our experience.

7. Therefore this Awareness is the constant substratum in which all things appear to arise, exist and subside. In addition, all living

things rely on Awareness of their environment to exist and their behaviour is directly affected by this. At the level of living cells and above this is self-evident, but it has been shown that even electrons change their behaviour when (aware of) being observed! Thus this Awareness exists at a deeper level than body/mind (and matter/energy[101]) and *we are this Awareness*!

8. This does not mean that at a surface level we are not the mind and body, for they arise in, are perceived by and subside back into Awareness, which is the deepest and most fundamental level of our being. However, if we choose to identify with this deepest level – Awareness - (the perceiver) rather than the surface level, mind/body (the perceived), then thoughts and sensations are seen for what they truly are, just ephemeral objects which come and go, leaving Awareness itself totally unaffected.

9. Next investigate this Awareness itself to see whether its properties can be determined.
Firstly what is apparent is that this Awareness is effortlessly present and effortlessly aware. It requires no effort by the mind/body and thoughts and sensations cannot make it vanish however hard they try.

---

[101] The theory of relativity, and string theory, show that matter and energy are synonymous.

10. Next, this Awareness is choicelessly present and choicelessly aware. Once again it requires no choice of the mind/body and they cannot block it however they try. For example, if you have a toothache there is effortless Awareness of it and the mind/body cannot choose for this not to be the case. You may think that this is bad news but it is not so: can you imagine if you had to make a choice whether you would like to be aware of every sensation that the body experiences? In fact be grateful that there is no effort or choice involved for Awareness just to be - such ease and simplicity - which is not surprising for you are this Awareness!

11. It can be seen then, that for each of us this Awareness is omnipresent; we never experience a time or place when it is not present. Once again be grateful that the mind/body is never required to search for this Awareness; it is just always there, which of course is not surprising for at the deepest level we are this Awareness.

12. Next, notice that this Awareness is absolutely still for it is aware of the slightest movement of body or mind. For example, we all know that to be completely aware of what is going on around us in a busy environment we have to be completely still, just witnessing the activity.

13. In the same vein this Awareness is totally silent as it is aware of the slightest sound and the smallest thought.

Investigation of Experience

14. In fact this Awareness is totally without attributes for all attributes occur in and are noticed by their lack, i.e. sounds occur in silence, exist in silence, are noticed by their contrast to silence, and disappear back into silence; forms occur in space, exist in space, are noticed by their contrast to space, disappear back into space, and so on.

15. It can be easily seen that this Awareness is totally pure; it is unaffected by whatever occurs in it, in the same way that a cinema screen is unaffected by any movie shown on it, however gross or violent. In fact no 'thing' can taint Awareness; for by definition Awareness cannot be affected by any 'thing', as all 'things' are just ephemeral objects which appear in, exist in and finally disappear back into Awareness, the constant subject.

16. This Awareness is omniscient; everything appears to arise in it, to exist in it, is known by it and to subside back into it.

17. Finally, it seems that this Awareness is forever radiant; it illuminates whatever occurs in it, thus the mind can see it, i.e. become conscious of it.

18. When one identifies with this Awareness, there is nothing (in terms of enlightenment or Awakening) to achieve, or struggle towards, for how can one achieve what one already is?

All that is required is for the mind to recognize that one is this Awareness.

19. When one identifies with this Awareness there is nothing to find, for how can one find what cannot be lost? All that is required is for the mind to stop overlooking what is always present, that which perceives the mind and body.

20. When one identifies with this Awareness, there is nothing to desire, long for or get, for how can one get what already is? All that is required is for the mind to realize that which one already is: pure Awareness.

So now we have reached the 'Pure, radiant, still, silent, omnipresent, omniscient, ocean of effortless, choiceless, attributeless Awareness' which we all are! Give up all striving, seeking and desiring, and just identify with This which you already are. Identification with This, rather than with body/mind (thought/sensations), gives instant peace, for Awareness is always still and silent, totally unaffected by whatever appears in it.

Although we, in essence, are 'The pure, radiant, still, silent, omnipresent, omniscient, ocean of effortless, choiceless, attributeless Awareness' it is impossible to experience this: we can know it or realize it but it is beyond the realm of experience. This is because all experience appears in This, exists in This and dissolves back into This. In much the same way that you do not see the cinema screen whilst the movie is playing, this pure screen of Awareness cannot be seen by the mind, i.e. experienced, whilst the movie of mind/body is playing on it. The only way it is possible to see the screen is when no movie is playing, but as *experience is the movie* this pure screen of Awareness is always outside of the realm of experience.

However, recognition of oneself as this 'pure, radiant, still, silent, omnipresent, omniscient, ocean of effortless, choiceless, attributeless, Awareness' may evoke many experiences such as bliss, joy, relaxation (what a relief that there's no individual 'me me me'), a lifting of a great burden, i.e. enlightenment in the literal sense of the word, universal love etc. These experiences vary greatly from person to person and are ultimately irrelevant as the recognition and realization of one's own essential nature is the crucial factor for attaining freedom.

Note that although we cannot experience our essence, we can absolutely know it* just as we know, without a doubt, that the screen is there (when we watch a movie). Then however terrifying, gripping or moving the movie is we are not shaken because we know it is a movie. We still enjoy it, in fact we enjoy it even more, because it is just pure entertainment and we are not totally identified with it. In the same way, once we know our essential nature, life can be seen as a movie and enjoyed as such without identifying ourselves as being trapped in it. Thus, although we cannot experience our essence, once we recognize it all of our experiences are transformed by no longer identifying with them but just enjoying them, or accepting them as ephemeral states which come and go. When viewed like this, thoughts and sensations lose their power to overwhelm us, as we stop buying into them as indicators of who or what we are. They are just like waves on the ocean or clouds in the sky, which appear and disappear leaving the ocean or the sky unaffected.

*Just as you could not see a movie without the screen, you could not experience anything without Awareness, for without that what would there be to experience? For without that we would see nothing (there would be no Awareness of what was seen), hear nothing, feel nothing, taste nothing, smell nothing and not know our own thoughts! In fact, experience on any level would not be possible.[102]

---

[102] C. Drake, *Beyond The Separate Self,* 2009, Tomewin, p.18-25

Addendum

Love Loving Itself

This is a powerful practice for 'sensing' the Absolute which has no reference in it to the imaginary separate self. I recommended this to a reader who was continually beset with his own 'story' and here is the outcome:

Hi Colin,

I'm doing beautifully since I seriously started doing the "Love Loving Itself" exercise several times a day. I'm not certain precisely when a "shift" occurred, but my true nature as Awareness is now perceived with much greater clarity and consistency than the endless and unmerciful "story of me". Ironically, this truth has been what I am since my very birth, right in front of my nose!

With Love and Thanks,

XXXX

Love Loving Itself

Here is a practice for 'sensing' the Absolute, through which the lover - pure Awareness, consciousness at rest – and the beloved – the manifest universe, cosmic energy, consciousness in motion – can 'know' and love each other. Thus the Absolute, consciousness in both modes, can know and love Itself.

Lie, or sit, in the most comfortable position you can possibly find, with your eyes closed. Make sure that the phone is off the hook and that the 'do not disturb' sign is on the door.

- 1/ Notice the sensations (and feelings) in, and on the surface of, the body. Sink into these sensations, really luxuriate in them as much as possible. Ignore all other sense impressions and thoughts except these sensations.

(If it appeals you may mentally repeat *Feeling you my love* as you do this.)

Realize that these occur, are detected by the nervous system, and are then 'seen' by Awareness – i.e. you become 'aware' of them.

So the body/mind is an instrument through which Awareness- consciousness at rest, the lover – can feel the external world – consciousness in motion, the beloved.

2/ Notice the sounds, occurring in the body and the room. Ignore all other sense impressions and thoughts except these sounds.

(If it appeals you may mentally repeat *Hearing you my love* as you do this.)

Realize that these occur, are detected by the ears, and are then 'seen' by Awareness – i.e. you become 'aware' of them.

So the body/mind is an instrument through which Awareness-consciousness at rest, the lover – can hear the external world – consciousness in motion, the beloved.

3/ Notice the aromas occurring in the room. Ignore all other sense impressions and thoughts except these aromas.

(If it appeals you may mentally repeat *Smelling you my love* as you do this.)

Realize that these occur, are detected by the nose, and are then 'seen' by Awareness – i.e. you become 'aware' of them.

So the body/mind is an instrument through which Awareness-consciousness at rest, the lover – can smell the external world – consciousness in motion, the beloved.

4/ Notice the tastes, occurring in the mouth. Ignore all other sense impressions and thoughts except these tastes.

(If it appeals you may mentally repeat *Tasting you my love* as you do this.)

Realize that these occur, are detected by the taste buds, and are then 'seen' by Awareness – i.e. you become 'aware' of them.

So the body/mind is an instrument through which Awareness-consciousness at rest, the lover – can taste the external world – consciousness in motion, the beloved.

5/ Open your eyes and notice what is seen. Ignore all other sense impressions and thoughts except these sights.

(If it appeals you may mentally repeat *Seeing you my love* as you do this.)

Realize that these occur, are detected by the eye, and are then 'seen' by Awareness – i.e. you become 'aware' of them.

So the body/mind is an instrument through which Awareness-consciousness at rest, the lover – can see the external world – consciousness in motion, the beloved.

6/ Close your eyes and notice the thoughts, occurring in the mind. Ignore all sense impressions just noticing the thoughts.

(If it appeals you may mentally repeat *Thinking of you my love* as you do this.)

Realize that these occur, are detected by the mind, and are then 'seen' by Awareness – i.e. you become 'aware' of them.

So the body/mind is an instrument through which Awareness-consciousness at rest, the lover – can contemplate the external world – consciousness in motion, the beloved.

7/ Notice the mental images occurring in the mind. Ignore all sense impressions just noticing these images.
(If it appeals you may mentally repeat *Imagining you my love* as you do this.)
Realize that these occur, are detected by the mind, and are then 'seen' by Awareness – i.e. you become 'aware' of them.

So the body/mind is an instrument through which Awareness-consciousness at rest, the lover – can imagine the external world – consciousness in motion, the beloved.

8/ Therefore the body/mind is an instrument through which Awareness- consciousness at rest, the lover – can experience, engage with and enjoy the external world – consciousness in motion, the beloved.

9/ To put this another way the body/mind – itself an ephemeral manifestation of consciousness in motion, the beloved – is an instrument, or conduit, through which the lover can 'know' and love the beloved.

<u>This is the end of the first phase, that of the lover loving the beloved.</u>

10/ Now notice that through this practice you are 'aware of Awareness'. This means that the mind notices the presence of Awareness. So this is the beloved noticing the lover.
Next investigate this Awareness so that the beloved can 'get to know' the lover better:

11/ Observe whether any effort is required to be aware of any thought/mental image/sensation.

This readily reveals that this Awareness is effortlessly present and effortlessly aware... It requires no effort by the mind/body and they cannot make it vanish however much effort they apply.

12/ Observe whether there is any choice in becoming aware of thoughts/mental images/sensations.

This also reveals that this Awareness is choicelessly present and choicelessly aware. Once again, it requires no choice of the body/mind and they cannot block it however they try. i.e. If you have a toothache there is effortless Awareness of it and the mind/body cannot choose for this not to be the case. You may think that this is bad news but that is not the case, can you imagine if you had to make a choice whether you would like to be aware for every sensation that the body experiences! In fact be grateful that there is no effort or choice involved for Awareness just to be...such ease and simplicity...which is not surprising for, at the deepest level, you are this Awareness!

13/ Observe whether you can ever experience a time or place when Awareness is not present. Even during sleep there is Awareness of dreams, the quality of the sleep, and bodily sensations, in that if a noise is loud enough or a feeling (of pain or discomfort for instance) is strong enough it will bring the mind back to the conscious state, i.e. One will wake up... The natural conclusion to this is that for each of us Awareness is omnipresent, i.e. always present. Once again be grateful that the mind/body is never required to search for this Awareness, it is just always there, which of course is not surprising for one is this Awareness.

14/ Next notice that this Awareness is absolutely still for it is aware of the slightest movement of body or mind. For example we all know that to be completely 'aware' of what is going on around us in a busy environment we have to be completely still, just witnessing the activity.

15/ In the same vein this Awareness can be 'seen' to be totally silent as it is aware of the slightest sound, the smallest thought. The natural conclusion to be drawn is that Awareness is always in a state of perfect peace for complete stillness and total silence is perfect peace.

16/ Notice that Awareness is omniscient, in that every thought/mental image/sensation appears in it, exists in it, is known by it, and disappears back into it. Before any particular thought or sensation there is effortless Awareness of 'what is' (the sum of all thoughts and sensations occurring at any given instant), during the thought or sensation in question there is effortless Awareness of it within 'what is', and then when it has gone there is still effortless Awareness of 'what is'.

17/ Finally notice that every thought/mental image/sensation is 'seen' by the 'light' of Awareness, i.e. Awareness is radiant.[103]

---
[103] C. Drake, *Beyond the Separate Self,* 2009, Tomewin, p.20-22

Love Loving Itself

So now we have reached the 'Radiant, still, silent, omnipresent, omniscient, ocean of effortless, choiceless, Awareness' (the Absolute without form or attributes) which, at the deepest level, we all are!
Thus the mind, an expression of the beloved, has come to 'know' (more about) Awareness, the lover.

Therefore, the body/mind - itself an ephemeral manifestation of consciousness in motion, the beloved – is an instrument, or conduit, through which the lover can 'know' and love the beloved, and through which the beloved can 'know' and love the lover. Thus the Absolute, consciousness, the union of lover and beloved, can love itself in both 'modes' – at rest or in motion – each 'mode' loving the other.

Feeling you my love.
Hearing you my love.
Smelling you my love.
Tasting you my love.
Seeing you my love.
Imagining you my love.
Thinking of you my love.
Knowing you my love.
Loving you my love.

Love Loving Itself

In which the 'doer' is pure Awareness, the lover, and that which is being addressed is the manifestation, the beloved. The instrument, body/mind, itself an ephemeral manifestation of the beloved, is the conduit through which love is loving itself.

Feeling you my love.
Hearing you my love.
Smelling you my love.
Tasting you my love.
Seeing you my love.
Imagining you my love.
Thinking of you my love.
Knowing you my love.
Loving you my love.

As you arise from this exercise let it continue, effortlessly, as long as it may, treating every thought and sensation with, and as, love. This will ultimately culminate in being totally in love with existence itself, in which there is nothing but love …

Just to show that this is not an exercise which requires that one be a spiritual adept there is a story about one of the first soviet cosmonauts which illustrates this. It seems that some external equipment on the sputnik became loose and was continually knocking on the windscreen. This was driving him mad and he thought that he would not be able to handle it for the long period he would be orbiting the earth. However, he then had the realization that all he had to do was to learn to love this sound ... which he did and this solved the problem!

In this there can be no separate 'saying',
The universe is the Lover and Beloved playing.
What appears to us as 'you' and 'me',
Are wondrous instruments, of the Beloved, Thee.

Between The Unmanifest and Manifestation,
There can never be any separation.
For the Lover and Beloved are already one,
Dancing the creation just for fun!

The Author – A short spiritual biography

I was born into a strict, but joyful, Methodist family. From the ages of 11-17 I was sent to a Methodist boarding school, which I left with the conviction that organized Christianity was not for me. I could see that what Christ said about living was wonderful, but that the church did not really promote his teachings rather concentrating on him as our 'saviour' and on the purportedly 'miraculous' facets of his life. It was also very apparent that many so called Christians were not interested in practicing what he taught. This was now 1965 and living in central London during the years of flower-power I experimented with various hallucinogens, finding them very beneficial for opening my subconscious which allowed years of conditioning to pour out. This left me feeling totally 'cleansed' and unburdened, ready to start life anew in a spirit of investigation as to the nature of reality. The psychedelic states also presaged, gave a glimpse of, mystical states which I suspected were attainable through spiritual practices. I then embarked on a study of Gurdjieff and Ouspensky which I found absolutely fascinating and was convinced that self-realization was the purpose of life. However, they made the process sound so onerous that (being young, foot-loose and fancy-free) I decided to shelve the whole project temporarily.

It was not until eight years later that I resumed the spiritual search when Janet (my partner) introduced me to my first yoga-teacher, Matthew O'Malveny, who inspired us by quoting passages from the Upanishads,

Dhammapada, and other scriptures during the class. He also emphasized the importance of relaxation and meditation. There followed a few years of investigating various spiritual paths including a prolonged dalliance with the Brahma Kumaris (Raja Yoga) whose meditations were wonderful, but whose dogma was very hard to take. We then moved into the country to start a pottery and immersed ourselves in Satyananda Yoga, an organization which had no dogma but taught a wide range of yogic practices. We were both initiated into *karma sannyas* by Swami Satyananda and adopted a yogic lifestyle consisting of asanas, pranayama, yoga nidra, meditation, kirtan and vegetarianism.

During this time I was at a silent retreat when I happened to pick up a volume entitled *The Gospel of Ramakrishna* which introduced me to this amazing being who practiced many spiritual paths, within Hinduism and also Islam and Christianity, discovering that they all lead to the same result. He was then approached by many devotees from these various paths all of whom he was able to teach in their own path, whilst emphasizing the harmony of religions. A few years later I was lucky enough to find an erudite nun in the Sarada Ramakrishna Order, based in Sydney, who initiated me into the worship of this amazing being. This entailed two to three hours of daily meditation, *japa* (mantra repetition) during daily activities, reading every word said by or written about him, including daily readings of *The Gospel of Sri Ramakrishna*, and chanting. I continued this sadhana quite happily for ten years.

Then in 1996 I encountered a disciple of Sri Ramana Maharshi, Gangaji, who said 'Stop! Be still, you are already That'. The message being that the effort and search were masking that which is always present; all that was required was to 'stop' and see what is always here. After many years of struggle and effort this news came like a breath of fresh air and I glimpsed the essence, that undeniable ever-present reality. This was followed by a seven day silent retreat which resulted in my first 'Awakening', and also in an ecstasy that slowly faded over the following year.

This and my first book *Beyond the Separate Self, The End of Anxiety and Mental Suffering* came about from the realization that occurred then and has matured over the following years. During this time I wrote a series of articles, for an e-mail news group, based on my meditations and contemplations, around which these books are based. At the same time I have also completed an honours degree in comparative religion and philosophy, using the insights gained by my spiritual practices to inform my essays. Some of these essays were adapted to include as chapters in these books.

Glossary

Advaita: non-dual.

Anatta: no self.

Anicca: impermanence.

Arhat: one who seeks personal enlightenment so as to attain *Nirvana* and avoid rebirth.

Atman: Brahman within each individual, that portion of the Absolute in each person.

Avatar: an incarnation of an aspect of the Godhead.

Avidya: spiritual ignorance.

Ayin: the nothingness from which 'everything emerges ... and eventually returns there'.

Bhumi: spiritual stage on the Bodhisattva Path.

Bodhicitta: Awakening or enlightenment.

Bodhisattva: one who seeks full enlightenment so as to aid others to do the same.

Brahman: the all-pervading transcendental Absolute Reality.

Darshan: the blessing or purification felt in the presence of holiness.

Dhamma (Buddhist): duty, following the Buddha's teachings to achieve *nirvana*.

Dharma (Hindu): duty, the criterion which is used to decide whether an action is right or wrong.

Dharmakaya: The Absolute Unmanifest Reality that is 'Aware Nothingness'.

Dvaita: dualist school of Vedantic philosophy proposed by Madhva.

Ein sof (or *En-Sof*): the infinite nothingness, the source and final resting place of all things.

Fana: absorption into the Absolute, which al-Junaid of Baghdad interpreted as 'dying to self'.

Hinayana: the 'small vehicle', a derogatory term coined by the Mahayanists for the path of those who seek personal liberation, the Arhats.

Japa: the practice of repeating one of the names of God.

Jiva: the individual self which houses the Atman, and which undergoes rebirth until self-realization (that atman *is* Brahman) occurs.

Kali: the Divine Mother, creator, preserver and destroyer. Sakti, cosmic energy, consciousness in motion.

Kandhas: the five aggregates (form, feeling, perception, mental fabrications and consciousness) which according to the Buddhists make up a human being.

Karma, Kamma: the merit or demerit accrued by your actions and thoughts which determine your present and future lives.

Krishna: an incarnation of Vishnu, the 'preserver'.

Lila: the divine play or manifestation, consciousness in motion.

Mahayana: the 'great vehicle' capable of carrying many people to liberation, as a bodhisattva is one who vows not to enter into the final *nirvana* until all creatures are liberated.

Mara: mind-created demons.

Maya: The power of Brahman, which supports the cosmic illusion of the One appearing as the many.

Moksa: liberation from the wheel of birth and death, self-realization, enlightenment.
Nama: name.
Namah: salutations (to).
Nirvana: Buddhist word for *moksa*, enlightenment, Awakening.
Nitya: the Ultimate Reality, the eternal Absolute.
Om: Brahman 'The Impersonal Absolute'; but is also the Logos, The Word, and the 'Ground of Being', in which all manifestation arises, exists and subsides.
Paramitas: perfections to be attained on the Bodhisattva Path.
Prakriti: the manifestation, nature.
Purusa: the witnessing consciousness, or awareness, according to Samkhya unique to each individual.
Rigpa: pure awareness which is 'the nature of everything'.
Sakti: cosmic energy, consciousness in motion.
Samkhya: philosophy proposed by Kapila which posited two fundamental principles, Purusa and Prakriti, as the source of all things.
Samsara: the wheel of birth, life, death and rebirth.
Satchitananda: existence (*sat*), consciousness (*chit*), bliss (*ananda*).
Satsang: association with Truth, normally with a guru or spiritual master.
Sefirot: the stages of divine being and aspects of divine personality.
Siva: universal consciousness when it is at rest, aware of every movement occurring in it, which is 'pure awareness'.
Sunyata: The void, formless awareness, aware nothingness
Tagatha: the Buddha.

The Tao: the ultimate principle; the source, which grows and nurtures all things.

Upanishads: the last works of the Vedas, in which ritual was supplanted by the personal and mystical experiencing of the Absolute (Brahman).

Vedanta: philosophy based on the books at 'the end of the Vedas' i.e. The Upanishads.

Bibliography

Books:

Anderson C., 'Pain and it's Ending', 1999, Curzon Press, Richmond.
Barks C. *The Essential Rumi*, 1995, Penguin, London.
Bataille G., 'Inner Experience', in Phwg313 *Unit Resources*, 2005, UNE, Armidale.
Bataille G., 'Radio National Encounter', in Phwg313 *Unit Resources*, 2005, UNE, Armidale.
Choong M., 'RELS305/405 Buddhism: A History', 2004, UNE, Armidale
Conze, E. 'Buddhist Scriptures', 1959, Penguin, Hammondsworth.
Drake, C. *Beyond The Separate Self*, 2009, Awakening and Beyond Publications, Tomewin
Drake, C. *A Light Unto Your Self*, 2011, Awakening and Beyond Publications, Tomewin
Drake, C. *Awakening and Beyond*, 2012, Awakening and Beyond Publications, Tomewin
Drake, C. *Poetry From Beyond The Separate Self*, 2011, Awakening and Beyond Publications, Tomewin
Drake, C. *Poetry From A Light Onto The Self*, 2012, Awakening and Beyond Publications, Tomewin
Easwaran E. 'The Dhammapada', 1986, Nilgiri Press, Petaluma.
Friedlander P. 'Buddhism Past and Present', 2002, La Trobe University, La Trobe.
Gowans C., 'The Philosophy of the Buddha', 2003, Routledge, London.
Gray F., 'Essentialism, Social Constructionism and The Divine, in *Phwg313 Unit Notes*, 2005, UNE, Armidale.
Gyatso, G.K., *Ocean of Nectar*, 1995, Tharpa Publications, London

Irigaray L., 'Elemental Passions', in *Phwg313 Unit Resources*, 2005, UNE, Armidale.
Irigaray L., 'Sexes and Genealogies', in *Phwg313 Unit Resources*, 2005, UNE, Armidale.
Harvey P., 'An Introduction to Buddhism', 1990, Cambridge Uni Press, Cambridge.
Horner I.B., 'The Middle Length Sayings Vol.11, 1989, Oxford Uni Press, Oxford.
Noys B., 'Radio National Encounter', in Phwg313 *Unit Resources*, 2005, UNE, Armidale.
Porete M., 'The Mirror of Simple Souls', in Phwg313 *Unit Resources*, 2005, UNE, Armidale.
Sells M., *Mystical Languages of Unsaying*, 1994, University of Chicago Press, Chicago.
Sw. Saradananda, *Sri Ramakrishna the Great Master*, 1979, Ramakrishna Math, Mylapore
Watts A., 'The Way of Zen', 1957, Pantheon Books, New York.
Williams P., 'Buddhist Thought', 2000, Routledge, London.

Internet Sites:

Bataille G. *Eroticism* in
pers-www.wlv.ac.uk/~fa1871/battext.html
www.richmondreview.co.uk/features/gargett01.html
Irigaray, *Spiritual Tasks of Our Times*, in www.unites.uqamca/religiologiques/21/21abstracts.html
Luce Irigaray and the Advent of the Divine, Feb 1999, Pacifica (Magazine) from:
http://dlibrary.acu.edu.au/staffhome/dacasey/Luce%20Irigaray%20and%20the%20Advent%20of%20the%20Divine.html

Index

A

A Light Unto Your Self (Drake), 10, 20, 34, 56–57, 147, 152–154
Absolute, The, 130, 133, 144. *see also* awareness
   attributes of, 140
   and awareness, 27, 28, 29, 199
   and *Brahman*, 146
   and consciousness, 149, 157
   duality within, 138
   as experiential, 71
   as formless, 139
   and *Jnana* Yoga, 148
   as pure nature, 70
   sensing, 192
   as totality of being, 43
absolute zero, 45, 46–47
Adam and Eve, as story of separateness, 60–61
advaita vedanta, 146, 169
Alexander, Eben, 138, 140
anatta, 169, 172, 176, 177, 178
anger, overcome by patience, 80
anicca, 172, 175, 177, 178
annihilationism, 177
astrology, as promoting separateness, 53–54, 57–58, 93
Atheists, ten commandments for, 118–119
Atman, 115, 146, 147, 169
attachment, 175, 176
attack, personal, 130–131
avidya, 151, 177, 179
awakening
   and awareness, 24
   of Buddha, 173
   cultivation of, 98
   flip-flopping with sleep, 110, 113, 127
   as freeing, 24
   glimpses of, 112
   key to, 18
   and life as play, 56
   and miraculousness of all things, 101
   nature of, 87
   no end to, 20

obstacles to, 113–114
  and Open Way, 22
  paths to, 22
  personal attributes associate with, 119–120, 136
  resistance to, 40
  sharing of, 70–73
  sign of, 81
  and silence of the mind, 127
  simplicity of, 92
  and societal prejudice, 81
Awakening and Beyond (Drake), 34, 46, 49, 81, 99
Awakening By Becoming Aware of Awareness (poem by Colin Drake), 83–90
aware, definition of, 6
Aware Nothingness, as infinite potential energy, 49
awareness
  as the Absolute, 27
  all things appearing in, 28
  and awakening, 10, 24. *see also* awakening
  of Awareness, 5–6, 30, 84, 196
  body/mind as instrument of, 192–201
  as *Brahman*, 146
  choicelessness of, 186, 197
  as common to all, 142–143
  as core of one's being, 112
  defined, 9
  desirelessness of, 188
  as doer, 200
  as effortless, 19, 23, 113, 184–189, 197–198
  and emotions, 33–34
  and enjoyment, 98
  and equanimity, 9–10
  as essence, 189–190
  and experience, 183–189
  identification with, 66–67, 76–77, 80, 81, 141, 185
  investigation of, 30, 183–188. *see also* investigation, direct
  and *Jnana* Yoga, 148
  as lover, 200
  and meaning, 100
  meanings of, 4–6
  mergence with, 161
  and mindfulness, 180
  and nonduality, 24–25
  and Ockham's Razor, 95
  omnipresence of, 186, 197

omniscience of, 187, 198
as presence, 6–9
properties of, 89–90
purity of, 187
radiance of, 187, 198–199
relaxing into, 23, 95
Rumi's description of, 9
as screen, 7, 188–189
and seeing things as they are, 6, 8–9
and sensations, 7
silence of, 186, 198
standing as, 66–67, 185
stillness of, 47, 146, 186, 198
as substratum, 184–185
and termination of mental programs, 109
as This, 189
and thought compared (chart), 17
of what is, 9
as what we are, 185
as without attributes, 187
writing as a reminder of, 70–73
awareness of Awareness, 5–6, 30, 84, 196

B
Barks, Coleman, 94
Bataille, Georges
    and Christianity, 158
    and dark night of the soul, 160
    and death, 158, 160
    and despair, 159, 160
    and eroticism, 160
    Georges Bataille (Gargett), 158
    and God, 158
    Inner Experience (Bataille), 158, 159, 160, 166
    as lacking full understanding, 169
    and laughter, 159
    and letting go, 159
    mysticism of, 157, 158–161
    and nothingness, 159, 166
    and oneness, 158
    and Porete, Marguerite, compared to, 165–166
    Radio National Encounter, 159, 160
    and Rumi, compared to, 165–166

and separate "I", loss of, 158, 160–161
　　teaching summarized, 161
　　and thoughts, 159
　　and violence, 160–161
belief, as knowing, 27, 30
Beloved, as consciousness, 101–103. *see also* love
Beyond the Separate Self (Drake), 7–9, 19, 34, 40, 46, 72, 77, 123, 125–126, 190
Bhagavad Gita, 109
bhava-samadhi, 140
big bang, 46, 48, 49
Blake, William, 175
bliss, and enlightenment, 189
Bodhi Tree, 173
Bodhisattva Path, 80, 114, 124, 127
body/mind. *see also* ego; "I", separate; mind
　　and consciousness, 24
　　experience of, 184, 185
　　as an instrument of awareness, 192–201
bondage, of the mind, 114
Book of Discipline, The (Homer), 173, 174, 176, 178
Botton, Alain de, 118
Brahman, 28–29, 140, 141, 169. *see also* awareness; consciousness; God
　　as awareness, 29
　　as consciousness, 29
　　as *siva* and *sakti*, 149
Brahmin, 178
Brihadaranyaka Upanishad, 29
Buddha, 5, 72, 84, 112, 172–174, 179–181
　　awakening of, 173
　　life of, 172–173
Buddhism, 118, 124, 131, 152, 169. *see also* Buddha; Four Noble Truths
　　Dhammapada, 172
　　Eightfold Path, 172
　　Four Noble Truths, 172–181
　　and stream entry, 173
　　Theravada, 172
　　and Vedic diagnosis, 173–174
Buddhism (Harvey), 173
Buddhism, Past and Present (Friedlander), 174
Buddhism: A History, Lecture Notes (Choong), 172, 175, 176, 178, 180
Buddhist Thought (Williams), 175, 176, 177, 180

C

chariot, man compared to, 146–147
choicelessness of awareness, 186, 197
Christ, Jesus, 140
Christianity
   and loss of separate "I", 158
   sin and, 151
compassion, 95
Complete Works of Swami Vivekananda, The (Vivekananda), 115
consciousness. *see also* awareness; Brahman; God
   arisings from, 50
   as Beloved, 101–103
   and enjoyment, 98
   "I" as instrument of, 37
   identification with, 65, 66–67
   as *Kali*, 100
   and miraculousness of all things, 99, 101
   modes of, 24
   relating to itself, 57
   as Self, 37
   as *Siva*, 100
   as "what is", 53
cosmic energy, 24, 49–50
craving, 175–177. *see also* Four Noble Truths

D

Dalai Lama, 71–72, 136
dark night of the soul, 160
Dawnsong (poem by Colin Drake), 101–103
death, 161
   and eroticism, 160
   experienced while alive, 159
   of God, 158, 161
   knowledge of, 158
   as violent return to ecstasy, 160
depression, 43
desire for oneness, 158, 161
desirelessness of awareness, 187
despair, 158, 159, 160, 161
dhamma, 180
Dhammapada, 172, 176–177, 178, 180
Dhammapada, The (Easwaran), 114, 172, 177, 178, 180
dharma, 180

diagnosis, Vedic, 173–174
direct experience, 85
direct investigation. *see* investigation, direct
direct perception, 8–9
discrimination, 148
Divine, the, 157–169. *see also* Irigaray, Luce; Bataille, Georges; Porete, Marguerite
   defined, 157
   and female embodiment, 162–164
   and love, 164
   and nothingness, 165–166
doer, as awareness, 200
Drake, Colin, email address, 15
duality, 138, 140. *see also* "I", separate
dukkha, 152, 172, 174, 175, 177, 181

E

ecstasy, 158, 159, 160
effortlessness of awareness, 19, 23, 113, 184–189, 197–198
ego, 56. *see also* "I", separate; mind
   compared to personality, 65–66
   defending itself, 81
   defined, 62
   as misidentification, 63
   myth of, 65, 66, 143–144
Eightfold Path, 172, 180–181. *see also* Four Noble Truths
Elemental Passions (Irigaray), 164
email address of Colin Drake, 15
embodiment, female, 163
emotions, 33–34, 183–188. *see also* investigation, direct
empathy, 118, 119
enjoyment, 148–149
enlightenment. *see also* awakening; freedom; love; nirvana
   and bliss, 189
   of Buddha, 173
   factors of, 5, 84
   and seeing, 147
equanimity, 9–10, 99
Eroticism (Bataille), 160
eroticism, and letting go, 160
essence, our nature as, 189–190
Essential Rumi, The (Barks), 94, 165, 166, 167, 168
Essentialism, Social Constructionism and The Divine (Gray), 163

eternalism, 177
ethics, 117
experience
    investigation of, 183–188
    as a movie, 189, 190
experiential knowing, 17, 19, 84. *see also* investigation, direct

F

faith, 115
fear, question about, 33
feeling you my love (poem by Colin Drake), 199
feelings, 183–188. *see also* investigation, direct
female embodiment, and the Divine, 163
female issues regarding God, 161–162
fifth dimension, 97, 99
flip-flop between awake and asleep, 110, 113, 127
forgiveness, 118, 120
Four Noble Truths, 172–181
    anatta, 172, 176, 177, 178
    anicca, 172, 175, 177, 178
    and annihilationism, 177
    and attachment, 175
    and *avidya*, 177, 179
    and craving, 175–177
    dukkha, 172, 174, 175, 177, 181
    and eternalism, 177
    and grasping, 175
    Harvey, Peter, 177
    kandhas, 172, 175, 176
    King Milinda, 178
    liberating power of, 173
    Nagasena, 178
    nibbana, 172, 173, 176, 178, 179, 180, 181
    nirvana, 178
    right concentration, 181
    right effort, 180
    right mindfulness, 180
    right speech, 180
    right thought, 180
    right view, 179
    and self-attachment, 176
    and sensory-attachment, 176
    truth of arising of suffering, 175–177

truth of cessation of suffering, 177–179
truth of Eightfold Path, 180–181
truth of suffering, 174–175
and Vedic diagnosis, 172
Williams, Paul, 175
freedom, 112, 114, 115, 189
Friedlander, Peter, 174

G
Gangaji, 34
gender issues regarding God, 161–162
Georges Bataille (Gargett), 158
Gibran, Kahlil, 117
God, 161–165
   aspects of, 138, 139
   conventional view of, 168–169
   death of, 158, 161
   defined, 157
   and duality, 140
   gender issues regarding belief in, 161–162
   loss of, 158
   and love, 169
Gospel of Ramakrishna, The (Gupta), 28, 100, 114
Gowans, Christopher W., 177
grasping, 175
gratitude, 57
Gray, Francis, 163
Griffiths, Bede, 151
Guide to the Middle Way (Chandrakirti), 80

H
Hail Pure Aware Nothingness (poem by Colin Drake), 49–51
Hare-Krishna devotees, 27
Harvey, Peter, 177
hope, 118, 120
How To Know God (Isherwood), 147–148
Humanity, Our Place in the Universe (Drake), 72, 139
humour, 118, 120

I
"I", separate, 35–36
   and Adam and Eve story, 60–61

   death and letting go of the, 160
   and eroticism, 160
   identifying as, 66, 105, 158
   as instrument of consciousness, 37
   investigation of, 36–37
   and labeling oneself, 53–54
   letting go of, 159–160
   loss of, 158, 161, 166, 169
   and orgasm, 160
   as self-analysis, 42–43
   as self-referential, 35–36, 152
   sin as nurturing of the, 151, 152, 154–155
   and violence, 160–161
"ian(s)", 93
identification
   with awareness, 66–67, 185
   with consciousness, 65
   with mind, 125–126
   with separate "I", 66, 86, 105, 153, 158
   with things, 54
illness, Vedic diagnosis of, 173–174
illusion, 87, 109, 112. *see also* ego; "I", separate; mind
In this there can be no separate 'saying' (poem by Colin Drake), 201
ineffable, 130, 135–136
Inner Experience (Bataille), 158, 159, 160, 166
inner light, 147
inquiry. *see* investigation, direct
investigation, direct, 5, 10, 19, 36–37, 149. *see also* practices
   as attacking the root of the problem, 42
   as cure for psychological problems, 43
   of experience, 183–188
   lightness of, 23
   necessity of, 133
   need to repeat, 22–23
   ruthlessness of, 34, 40
   of sensations, 183–188
   suffering as trigger to, 23
   of thoughts, 183–188
Irigaray, Luce, 157
   and death of God, 161
   Elemental Passions, 164
   and female embodiment, 163
   and feminine Divine, 162–163, 169–170
   and Gray, Francis, 163

as lacking full understanding, 170
and love, 164
Luce Irigaray and the Advent of the Divine (Casey), 163
and nature, 163, 164
Sexes and Genealogies (Irigaray), 162, 164
Spiritual Tasks of Our Times (Irigaray), 163
and transcendence, 163, 164
uniqueness of, 167
and women's issues regarding God, 161–162
Isha Upanishad, 29
"isms", 92
"it(ies)", 93–94

J
Jesus, 140
jhanas, 181
Jnana, 18
Jnana Yoga, 148
joy, 114

K
Kahlil Gibran, 117
Kali, consciousness as, 100
kandhas, 172, 175, 176
karma, 97, 98, 99
Karma Yoga, 109
Katha Upanishad, 29, 146–147
Kena Upanishad, 29, 146
King Milinda, 178
kirtan, 97
knowing, 27, 148
Kondanna, and stream entry, 173
Krishna, Sri, 109

L
labels, danger of identifying with, 54, 92, 94–95. *see also* "I", separate; identification
Lamotte, Etienne, 172
laughter, upon experience of nothingness, 159
letting go of separate "I", 159–161
liberation, 148
light, inner, 147

lila, 148–149
loss of the separate "I", 158, 161, 166, 169
love
    as the Divine, 164
    as non-separateness, 53, 138
    practice for realizing, 192–201
lover, as awareness, 200
Luce Irigaray and the Advent of the Divine (Casey), 163

M

Maha Sattipatthana Sutta, 5
meditation, *vipassana*, 180. *see also* practices
Methodist upbringing, sin and, 151
methods. *see* practices
Milindapasha in Buddhist Scriptures (Conze), 178
mind, 17
    complexity of, 92, 95
    and concentration, 181
    as creating problems, 76, 125–127
    efficient use of, 105, 107, 109
    identification with, 125–126
    life shaped by, 114
    limitation of, 18–19
    as naked, 84
    negative feelings arising in, 123
    as object, 63
    and resistance to awakening, 40
    silence of, 127
    stillness of, 54, 56. *see also* practices
    and termination of programs, 109
    thinking and the, 75–77
    as a tool, 8
mind/body. *see* body/mind
mindfulness, 6, 180
miracles, 99, 101
Mirror of Simple Souls (Porete), 168
misidentification, 63, 92–95, 113. *see also* identification
moksha. see freedom
money, as motive for writing, 69
motion and stillness, 45, 47, 48, 49–50, 146
movie, experience as a, 189, 190
Mundaka Upanishad, 29
Mystical Languages of Unsaying (Sells), 166

mysticism of Georges Bataille, 158–161
Myth of Ego (Separation), The (poem by Colin Drake), 143–144

N
Nagarjuna, 80
Nagasena, 178
nature, perceived directly, 8–9
NDE, 138
near death experience, 138
negative thinking discussed, 75–77
neurosis, 35–36
nibbana, 172, 173, 176, 178. *see also nirvana*
nirvana, 152, 178. *see also* freedom; *nibbana*
nirvikalpa samadhi, 28, 30, 140
nitya, 148–149
nonduality, 24–25, 130–131, 139, 141
   questions for self-investigation, 134
non-separateness. *see* awareness; Brahman; consciousness; love; nonduality
nothingness
   and Divinity, 165–166
   laughter upon experience of, 159
   as letting go of the separate "I", 159
   things occurring relative to, 149, 159
noticing, 6–9, 113
Noys, Benjamin, 160–161
nurturing the separate self, 151, 152, 154–155. *see also* "I", separate

O
obstacles, to awakening, 113–114
Ocean of Nectar (Gyatso), 80
Ockham's Razor, applied to relaxing into awareness, 95
"ologies", 92–93
omnipresence of awareness, 186, 197
omniscience of awareness, 187, 198
oneness, 138
   as absolute zero, 47
   as all there is, 49
   desire for, 158
   and physics, 45
Open Way, 5, 22
orgasm, and letting go of the separate "I", 160
original sin. *see* sin

P

Pain and its Ending (Anderson), 172
Papaji, 34, 113
paradox, of duality/nonduality, 143–144
paths to awakening, 22, 36
patience, and overcoming anger, 80, 118, 120
personal attack, described, 130–131
personality, compared to ego, 66
Philosophy of the Buddha (Gowans), 173, 181
poems by Colin Drake
   Awakening By Becoming Aware of Awareness, 83–90
   Dawnsong, 101–103
   feeling you my love, 199
   Hail Pure Aware Nothingness, 49–51
   The Myth of Ego (Separation), 143–144
   There are many things that we are told, 55–57
   In this there can be no separate 'saying', 201
   Why Write About the Inevitable, 135–136
Poetry From A Light Unto Your Self (Drake), 35
Poetry From Beyond The Separate Self (Drake), 35, 139
politeness, 118, 120
Poonjaji (Papaji), 34, 113
Porete, Marguerite, 157, 165–166, 168
positive thinking discussed, 75–77
practices. *see also* investigation, direct
   experiencing presence, 6–9
   investigating experience, 183–188
   investigating the "I", 36–37
   love loving itself, 192–201
   noticing awareness of what is, 9
   noticing sensations, 6–9
   positive and negative thinking, 75–77
   realizing of suffering, 23
   relaxing into awareness, 23
   ruthlessness of, 34, 40
   seeing awareness as screen for thoughts, 141
   writing, 72
prejudice, addressed from awakening, 79–82
presence, experiencing, 6–9
problems in life, 76, 125–127
Proof of Heaven (Alexander), 138
Prophet, The (Gibran), 117
psychiatry, limitations of, 40–42

psychoanalysis, as misidentification, 63
psychotherapy, limitations of, 40–42
pure awareness. *see* awareness
purity of awareness, 187

Q
questions for nondualists, 134

R
racial prejudice, addressed from awakening, 79–82
radiance of awareness, 187, 198–199
Radio National Encounter (Battaile), 159, 160
Radio National Encounter (Noys), 161
Raja Yoga, 148
Ramakrishna, Sri, 20, 28, 100, 114, 139, 140
   and Divine Mother, 28
Ramakrishna, Sri, The Great Master (Saradananda), 140
Ramakrishna Vedanta Wordbook, A (Usha), 140
Ramana Maharshi, 30, 34
Ramana Maharshi (Osborne), 30
reality. *see* Absolute, The; awareness; Brahman; consciousness; God; nonduality; truth, discovering
realization. *see* awakening
re-identification, with the separate "I", 158
relativity, theory of, 185
relaxing into awareness, 23, 95
religion, 117–118
resistance to awakening, 40
Return to the Center (Griffiths), 151
right concentration, 181. *see also* Four Noble Truths
right effort, 180. *see also* Four Noble Truths
right mindfulness, 180. *see also* Four Noble Truths
right speech, 180. *see also* Four Noble Truths
right thought, 180. *see also* Four Noble Truths
right view, 179. *see also* Four Noble Truths
Rumi, 9, 94, 141, 165–168

S
sacrifice, 118, 120
sahaj samadhi, 30, 141
Sakti, 148
samadhi, 28, 30, 140, 141, 147

savikalpa samadhi, 140
screen, awareness as a, 7, 188–189, 190
seeing
    awareness as, 6
    difference between real and unreal, 147–148
    as noticing, 6–9, 113
Self. *see* consciousness; Absolute, The; awareness
self. *see* "I", separate
self-analysis, 42–43
self-attachment, 176
self-awareness, 118, 120
self-esteem, 62, 66–67
self-grasping, 35–36
self-identity. *see* "I", separate
self-image, as imaginary, 86
self-inquiry. *see* investigation, direct
self-realization. *see* awakening
self-referencing, 124
sensations, 6, 7, 56. *see also* investigation, direct
    investigation of, 183–188
sensible transcendent, of Irigaray, 163
separate "I". *see* "I", separate
Sexes and Genealogies (Irigaray), 162, 164
silence
    of awareness, 186, 198
    of the mind, 127
simplicity of awakening, 92, 95
sin
    as *avidya*, 151
    Christian upbringing and, 151
    defined by dictionary, 154
    mentioned in *Return to the Center* (Griffiths), 151
    as nurturing of the separate "I", 151, 152, 154–155
    original, 37, 151
    questioned by reader, 60
    subjective aspects of, 154
Siva, consciousness as, 100, 148
sophist, 135, 136
soul, 115
Spiritual Tasks of Our Times (Irigaray), 163
standing as awareness, 66–67, 185. *see also* awareness
sthitha samadhi, 28
stillness, 45, 47, 48, 49–50, 146, 186, 198
stream entry, 173

string theory, 185
suffering, 23, 113, 114. *see also* Buddha; Buddhism; ego; Four Noble Truths; "I", separate; mind
   and Buddha, 172–173
   as nurturing of the separate self, 152
suicide, thoughts of, 135
Svetasvetara Upanishad, 29, 147

T
Tantra Yoga, 148–149
Tao, 5, 69, 135
Tao Te Ching, 117, 135
ten commandments for virtuous Atheists, list of, 118–119
That. *see* awareness; consciousness
The Mirror of Simple Souls who are Annihilated (Porete), 166, 168
theory of relativity, 185
Theravada, 172
There are many things that we are told (poem by Colin Drake), 55–57
This. *see* awareness; consciousness
thoughts, 56. *see also* investigation, direct
   awareness as screen for, 141
   and awareness compared, 17
   investigation of, 183–188
   letting go of, 161
   noticing, 113
   positive and negative discussed, 75–77, 114
   right thought, 180
   of suicide, 135
   taking seriously, 159
time, elasticity of, 106–107
transcendence
   and female embodiment, 163
   of Irigaray, Luce, 163, 164
   of Porete, Marguerite, 168
   as rooted in nature, 163
truth, discovering, 84. *see also* awareness; Four Noble Truths

U
Upanishads, 28
   Brihadaranyaka, 29
   Isha, 29
   Katha, 29, 146, 147
   Kena, 29, 146

Mundaka, 29
Svetasvetara, 29, 147
Upanishads (Easwaran), 29

V
Vedanta, 146, 169
Vedic diagnosis, 173–174
violence, and letting go of the separate "I", 160–161
vipassana, 180
Vivekananada, Swami, 82, 114–115

W
Way, the, 117
Way of Zen, The (Watts), 174
"what is"
 defined, 53
 experiencing, 54. *see also* practices
Why Write About the Inevitable (poem by Colin Drake), 135–136
Williams, Paul, 175, 176
witness, 17
women's issues regarding God, 161–162
writing
 motives for, 69–70, 72, 136
 practice of, 72
 as sharing awakening, 70–73

Y
Yoga
 Jnana, 148
 karma, 109
 Raja, 147, 148
 sutras of Patanjali, 118, 148
 Tantra, 148–149
Yoga Aphorisms of Patanjali (Prabhavananda), 148

Lightning Source UK Ltd.
Milton Keynes UK
UKHW011529140322
400044UK00002B/395